A THOUSAND AND ONE DELIGHTS

by the same author
DAYS OF THRILLS AND ADVENTURE

ALAN G. BARBOUR

A Thousand and One Delights

COLLIER BOOKS, New York, New York

COLLIER-MACMILLAN LTD., London

The Macmillan Company
866 Third Avenue, New York, N.Y. 10022
Collier-Macmillan Canada Ltd., Toronto, Ontario

A *Thousand and One Delights* is published in hardcover
by The Macmillan Company.

Library of Congress Catalog Card Number: 72-165568
First Collier Books Edition 1971
Printed in the United States of America

Dedicated to my mother,

MILDRED BERNADINE MARRIOTT,

with lasting love and gratitude

The author wishes to express his sincere thanks and appreciation to the individuals and organizations listed below who supplied, through the years, the stills and information which have made this book possible.

The Individuals:
Ernest Burns, John Cocchi, Edward Connor, Henry Kier, Al Kilgore, Ernie Kirkpatrick, Paula Klaw, Louis McMahon, Gray Morrow, James Robert Parish, Mark Ricci, Gene Ringgold, Stephen Sally, Chris Steinbrunner.

The Organizations:
Allied Artists-TV, Banner Films, Burroughs-Tarzan, Inc., Cinemabilia, Columbia Pictures Corp., Eagle-Lion Films, Empire Films, Fawcett Publications, Inc., Four Star International, Janus Films, Kier's, King Features Syndicate, London Films, Marvel Comics Group, MCA-TV, Medallion TV, The Memory Shop, MGM, MGM-TV, Monogram Pictures, Movie Star News, National Periodical Publications, Inc., National Telefilm Associates, Paramount Pictures, Paramount-TV, Premium Products, Inc., PRC, Republic Pictures Corp., RKO-Radio Pictures, Screen Gems, Inc., Street and Smith Publications, Twentieth Century-Fox, United Artists, United Artists Associated, United Features Syndicate, Inc., Universal Pictures Corp., Universal-International, Walter Reade-Sterling, Warner Bros, Warner Bros-Seven Arts, Inc.

With Special Thanks to:
Jean Barbour and Malcolm McPherson

Contents

PREFACE
xi

1 THE KING AND QUEEN
OF TECHNICOLOR
1

2 CHAMPS OF THE CHASE
15

3 BRING THEM BACK AGAIN . . .
AND AGAIN
29

4 AND THINGS THAT GO BUMP
IN THE NIGHT
45

5 THE BEST MEDICINE
61

6 THE FUN FACTORY
75

7 SATURDAYS ARE FOR THRILLS
87

8 MURDER FOR THE MASSES
103

9 DUSTY TRAILS TO ADVENTURE
121

10 NEW WORLDS TO CONQUER
135

11 MAN OF ACTION
149

12 THE HORN OF PLENTY
163

Preface

Remembering the days of one's moviegoing youth can be a pleasant and, at the same time, painful experience. We can conjure up wonderful images of hundreds of entertainment-laden afternoons spent sharing those worlds of pure escapism on the screen which were limited only by the capacities of our individual imaginations; but we all face an annoying enemy as we grow older called *maturity*, which attacks those very same imaginations and tries to convince us that much of what we saw and enjoyed as children was, like a sand castle before the waves, unable to stand the test of time. Unfortunately, like most film buffs, I have spent a good part of my life watching my two-dimensionally-created cinema world crumble bit by bit as each new screening of a long unseen, treasured childhood film revealed itself to be, for want of a better expression, simply awful!

However, though I may have scratched a great many films from my lists of all-time favorites, there still remain a great number of presentations that I feel have held up amazingly well through the years, and those, really, are what *this* book is all about. It is by no means a "history" of films of the forties, for that is too giant a task to cover in one small volume; rather, it is a kind of personal photographic record of what I like to call the "fun films" of that time—films which were largely escapist in nature, many of which turned out as what we now call B-films. On occasion some big-budget films will appear in these pages, as will films made in the thirties, simply because, through reissues during the next decade, they played an important part in my weekly moviegoing routine.

After my first book of movie nostalgia, *Days of Thrills and Adventure*, was published, one of the nicest things said about it was in the review in *Playboy* magazine: their reviewer stated simply that "the author's enthusiasm is contagious." More than anything else, *that* is what I hope to convey to the readers in this book as well—the *enthusiasm* I had as a youngster each time I made that weekly journey to my favorite theater to see the films you'll discover, perhaps for the first time, in these pages.

Jon Hall discovers that this lady is not his runaway fiancée but the evil
Queen of Cobra Island in *Cobra Woman* (Universal 1944).

I.

The King and Queen
of Technicolor

If I had to name the one series of films that most captured the escapist spirit of the films of the forties, I would unhesitatingly choose the six filmed-in-Technicolor Jon Hall—Maria Montez adventures turned out by Universal between 1942 and 1945. These were all action classics designed to entertain and thrill audiences who wanted to get their minds off the everyday problems of a world that seemed to be exploding around them. Just mentioning the name of Maria Montez can conjure up the most delicious memories of azure pools, eye-dazzling costumes, spellbinding action, and worlds that could only exist and be amplified in the minds of the true cinema addicts of those exciting moviegoing days.

The series got off to an extremely glamorous start with Walter Wanger's opulent production of *Arabian Nights* in late 1942. Very loosely based upon the famous tales, the story found Leif Erickson plotting to steal the throne from his brother, Jon Hall. After a murderous attempt on his life, Hall is rescued by the young Sabu (fresh from his personal triumph in *Jungle Book* earlier the same year) and Montez, who played the dancing girl Scheherazade. Montez, who was scheduled to marry Erickson, quickly lost her heart to Hall not knowing he was the rightful ruler. An important participant in the film's colorful chicanery was Edgar Barrier, who planned to force Montez to poison Erickson and thus gain the throne for himself. Needless to say, such devilment was justly rewarded when Barrier dispatched Erickson and then perished himself in a fiery screen finale. The one sour note in the

entire lavish production was the intrusion of banal comedy routines by Billy Gilbert, sneezing as usual, Shemp Howard, and others. It was interesting to note that Turhan Bey, who was to replace Hall as Montez's love interest in the final film of the series, had only a small role in this production as one of Barrier's treacherous henchmen.

A jewel-studded swimming pool was the central point of contention in *White Savage*. Portly Thomas Gomez, after twenty years of patient waiting, hoped to gain the glittering baubles from the Temple Island water tank by marrying Montez, who, as Princess Tahia, ruled the tiny paradise. Hall, playing a shark-hunter interested in acquiring fishing rights off the island, eventually wins the heart of Montez and discovers the secret cache of wealth—to the dismay of Gomez, who, in turn, kills the Princess's brother, played by Turhan Bey in spirited fashion, and frames Hall. Assisting Hall again was his friend and occasional nuisance, Sabu. The film featured a thrilling finale which found Gomez and his band of cutthroats dynamiting the outside wall of the pool, eventually causing tons of rock to fall upon the evil trespassers digging up the treasure. Unfortunately, most of the island seemed to be destroyed at the same time, but back-lot paradises bounce back quickly. It was all adventure in a grand style. Several years later stock footage from these sequences and others were used to create three chapter endings in the serial *Lost City of the Jungle*.

In *Ali Baba and the Forty Thieves* Hall was at

his dashing best as the grown-up son of the Caliph of Bagdad, whom Frank Puglia betrayed and had killed to ingratiate himself with the Mongol tyrant Hulagu Khan, portrayed beautifully by the leering, accented Kurt Katch. Montez, Puglia's daughter, had pledged her love to Hall in a blood ritual when they were children, but, believing him to have been killed at the time of his father's death, was now slated for marriage to the Mongol despot in order to save her treacherous father's life. Hall, portrayed as a youth by Scotty Beckett, stumbled across the treasure-laden secret cave of the forty thieves and, when discovered, announced he was the son of the slain Caliph and joined their band, eventually assuming leadership and converting them from thieves to avengers out to liberate Bagdad from the Mongols. Turhan Bey had his best role to date as Montez's faithful servant who joined the thieves in their campaign. Along for laughs was Andy Devine, who managed to be unobtrusively funny and had the pleasurable assignment of throwing a sword through the demon heart of Katch just as the devil was about to eliminate Hall at the end of a thrilling duel to the death. A highlight of the film was a breathtaking dance, backed by the exquisite music of Edward Ward, photographed from an overhead crane à la Busby Berkeley. One of the distinctive features of the entire series was the fluid use of the camera, and its capabilities were never more in evidence than here, with numerous travel and dolly shots to delight the viewer. *Ali Baba* is my personal favorite in the series, and most Montez aficionados find themselves frequently quoting lines from this film ("Rubies . . . blood red . . . for the people of Bagdad who stood in my way," uttered by Katch as he placed a necklace around Montez's throat, is a favorite). *Ali Baba* was also the longest of the series in running time, taking eighty-seven minutes to unfold its adventurous tale. With the exception of *Arabian Nights*, which ran eighty-six minutes, the other four films ran less than eighty minutes each. In those wartime days when color film was scarce because of military priorities, most color films were shot with virtually no padding to eat up unnecessary footage.

If one Montez was dazzling, then two had to be sensational, and Universal served us this doubledip of pleasure in *Cobra Woman*. In this tropical adventure Montez was captured on the eve of her wedding to Hall and taken to Cobra Island, where it was hoped that she would take over the throne then occupied by her evil twin sister, who had a singularly unpleasant habit of tossing friendly villagers into a nearby volcano as sacrifices. Hall and Sabu, who was making his final appearance in the series, naturally follow the kidnapped Montez to the island where they are captured by the High Priest, played skillfully by Edgar Barrier, whose villainy reaches its zenith when he fatally stabs the Queen Mother (Mary Nash) while a smoldering volcano erupts to bathe his crime in crimson brilliance. Montez accidentally kills her sister and takes her place, but is discovered by Barrier, who forces her to dance in the Cobra Ritual, something she didn't appear to enjoy too keenly but which we in the audience loved. Just in time, of course, Hall and Sabu are freed, and a terrific battle ensues as the volcano erupts anew causing scattered havoc. Lon Chaney, Jr., playing a friendly killer for a welcome change of pace, hurls Barrier into a pit full of spikes as a just reward for his superior show of master villainy.

The weakest film in the series was undoubtedly *Gypsy Wildcat*, primarily because of various excesses in the acting department. This colorful extravaganza of a band of gypsy performers combating an evil overseer found Douglas Dumbrille and Nigel Bruce, ordinarily two polished professionals, hamming and mugging their roles abominably. Montez was a gypsy dancing girl who in reality—and unbeknownst to her—was the heiress to a kingdom now ruled by despotic Dumbrille. Discovering the secret, Dumbrille captures her and plans a quick wedding in order to legalize his position. Hall was a Royal Emissary sent to prove a murder charge against Dumbrille, but nearly wound up being another of his victims while falling in love with Montez. Once again Edward Ward provided a musical score that enhanced the visual spectacle, and an exciting coach chase over treacherous mountain trails was extremely pleasurable to watch. Giving excellent back-up performances were Gale Sondergaard and Leo Carrillo as Montez's foster parents, while Peter Coe as Hall's rival for Montez's affection was, at best, only adequate.

By the time the last film in the series, *Sudan*, reached the screen, much of the magic was beginning to dissipate. Hall was putting on weight and was not quite as dashing as one would want a hero to be. The love-interest assignment was now turned over to Turhan Bey, who played a rebel leader living in a secret mountain hideout who was trying to free his people from the oppression imposed by George Zucco. Zucco plotted to have Montez, the rightful though misguided ruler, killed, but failed in the attempt when Bey rescued her and took her to his hidden retreat. Hall and pal Andy Devine went along for laughs and some adventure, but their days in the sun seemed over. The finale, one of the most exciting in the series, found Montez leading Zucco and his army up a winding mountain trail toward the hidden encampment. Mounted high above the trail was a series of rock-filled containers held closed by fastened ropes that were cut at the appropriate time, unleashing a torrent of death and destruction down upon the invading enemy. Naturally, Montez was spared and Zucco was rewarded with death for his supreme treachery.

With *Sudan* came the end of an immensely popular series of films which were frequently reissued either in pairs or matched up with other Universal color triumphs (like *The Phantom of the Opera*). No one would ever be bold enough to suggest that either Jon Hall or Maria Montez were first-rate actors, but they did have that certain magic when they appeared together that captured our hearts and imaginations.

Maria Montez in a publicity pose for *Cobra Woman* (Universal 1944).

Above: Jon Hall battles Leif Erickson in the final climactic duel to the death while Maria Montez remains a prisoner in *Arabian Nights* (Universal 1942). *Right:* Jon Hall won Maria Montez's love in *Arabian Nights* (Universal 1942) even though she had no knowledge that he was royalty in disguise. *Below:* Maria Montez in a publicity pose for *Arabian Nights*. (Universal 1942).

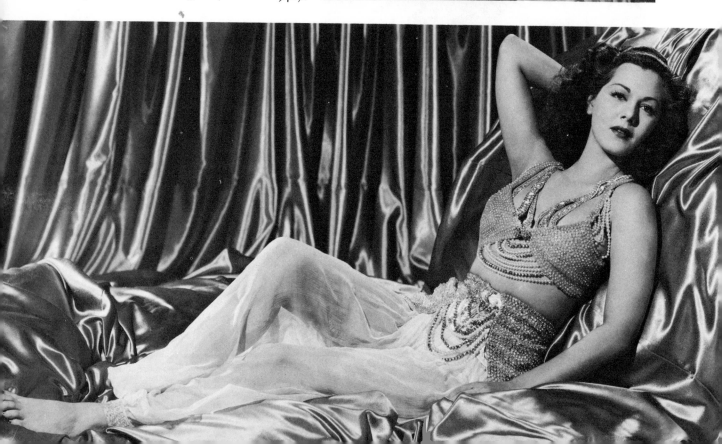

Top, left: Jon Hall and Sabu participated in a spectacular battle to escape from a slave gallery in *Arabian Nights* (Universal 1942). *Top, right:* Maria Montez in a publicity pose for *White Savage* (Universal 1943). *Left:* Jon Hall in a fanciful action shot from *Arabian Nights* (Universal 1942).

5

Opposite page, top: Technicians set up their equipment to photograph a scene for *White Savage* (Universal 1943) while Maria Montez and Jon Hall go over their dialogue. *Opposite page, bottom left:* Maria Montez leads Jon Hall to the Sacred Jeweled Pool in *White Savage* (Universal 1943). *Opposite page, bottom right:* Maria Montez is told that her brother has just been slain in *White Savage* (Universal 1943).

Left: Jon Hall and Maria Montez ham it up a little for the benefit of the cameraman in this publicity pose for *Arabian Nights* (Universal 1942). *Below:* Sabu's sudden dive into one of those beautiful azure back-lot pools is rewarded with this little surprise in *Arabian Nights* (Universal 1942).

Above: Turhan Bey has caught Ramsay Ames listening in on a conversation between himself and Maria Montez in *Ali Baba and the Forty Thieves* (Universal 1944). *Left:* Frank Puglia presents Maria Montez to bald-headed Kurt Katch in this scene from *Ali Baba and the Forty Thieves* (Universal 1944). *Below:* Kurt Katch as the Mongol tyrant Hulagu Khan in *Ali Baba and the Forty Thieves* (Universal 1944).

Below: Jon Hall decides to enter the well-guarded palace by placing his men in forty large vases which will supposedly be holding oil as a gift for the Khan's wedding in *Ali Baba and the Forty Thieves* (Universal 1944). *Right:* The spectacular overhead shots for *Ali Baba and the Forty Thieves* (Universal 1944) as well as for many other Universal adventures were filmed from this elaborate camera boom.

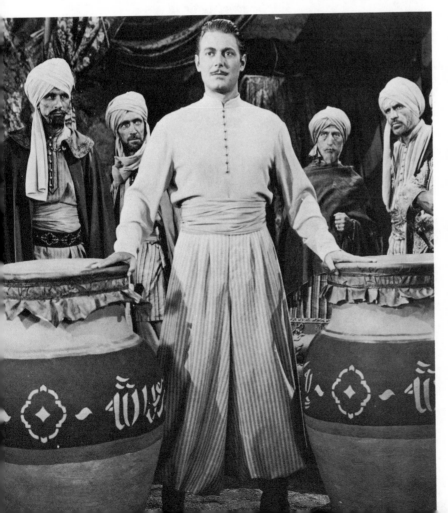

Top: Maria Montez in an exquisite close-up publicity shot for *White Savage* (Universal 1943). *Center:* Maria Montez regains the throne from her evil sister with the help of Lon Chaney, Jr., and Lois Collier in *Cobra Woman* (Universal 1944). *Bottom:* Edgar Barrier met his well-deserved end in *Cobra Woman* (Universal 1944) when Lon Chaney, Jr., threw him into a pit of spikes which was intended for Jon Hall and Sabu. This close-up scene is usually deleted from television screenings by touchy censors.

Left: Maria Montez in a publicity pose for *Gypsy Wildcat* (Universal 1944). *Below:* A little frivolous horseplay between Maria Montez and Jon Hall in *Gypsy Wildcat* (Universal 1944), the weakest of the six films in the series.

Left: Maria Montez in a publicity pose for the last film in the series, *Sudan* (Universal 1945).
Above: Andy Devine doesn't look too pleased with whatever Jon Hall has in mind to help Maria Montez in *Sudan* (Universal 1945).

Opposite page, top: Maria Montez and Jon Hall in a romantic interlude from *White Savage* (Universal 1943). *Opposite page, bottom:* Edgar Barrier tries to convince Maria Montez that a sacrifice must be made to the Volcano God in *Cobra Woman* (Universal 1944).

Lou Costello and Bud Abbott in their very first movie appearance in
One Night in the Tropics (Universal 1940). They were so successful with
their routines in the film that Universal signed them
to star in their very next film.

2.

Champs of the Chase

While the passing years have proved to me that *the* great comedy team in films was Stan Laurel and Oliver Hardy, during my youthful moviegoing I saw very little of them on the screen. On occasion some theater would book a rerun of *Blockheads* or *Swiss Miss*, but on the whole the rare glimpses I had of the comedic geniuses were in those abominations (which Laurel and Hardy both hated vehemently) turned out by Twentieth-Century-Fox (*Great Guns*, *Jitterbugs*, etc.). I had to wait over twenty years, until the sixties, to witness what classic comedy, Laurel and Hardy style, was like. However, I and my peer group did have our own comedy team—and on their own merits they were enormously popular and successful. They were, of course, Bud Abbott and Lou Costello.

Both Bud and Lou paid their dues in the Fraternity of Hard Knocks, moving slowly up the ladder of success through clubs, vaudeville, burlesque, radio, motion pictures and, finally, television. While appearing to rave reviews on the Kate Smith radio show in the late thirties, the boys were offered a screen contract to appear as second leads in Allan Jones's starring film, *One Night in the Tropics* (sometimes called *Caribbean Holiday*). Audience response was so good to this initial screen appearance of the boys in 1940 that the studio signed them to star immediately in *Buck Privates*. The rest was history. For over a decade the team worked together (but not without frequent off-screen break-ups, serious illnesses, etc.) to provide a generation of youngsters and adults with outstanding comedy films.

There are many who feel that *Buck Privates* was the pair's best film and all subsequent features merely anticlimactic follow-ups. The point is well taken, for the film certainly had many good things going for it. In addition to featuring two of their funniest routines, the "dice game" and "Army drill" bits, the film also had the advantage of utilizing the services of the popular Andrews Sisters, who sang two of their very best numbers, "I'll Be With You in Apple Blossom Time" and "You're a Lucky Fellow, Mr. Smith." (Most of the team's earlier films featured musical sequences, but these embellishments were left out of many of the later films in favor of straight comedy.) Although the classic routines were delightfully entertaining, I found myself usually laughing at the little throwaway lines (an example: Nat Pendleton as a boxing referee begins to count over a temporarily prostrate Costello, "Two, four, six, eight"; Lou asks anxiously, "What's wrong with one, three, five, seven?"; Pendleton replies, "I don't like them numbers. They're *odd!*") or the quickie bits—Abbott: "Lou, suppose you were forty and you were engaged to a girl who was ten." Costello: "Oh, boy, this is gonna be a pip!" Abbott: "Never mind. Now, you're four times older than that little girl. So you wait five years. You're forty-five and the girl is fifteen. Now you're only three times as old as that little girl. So you wait fifteen more years. The little girl is thirty and you're sixty. Now you're only twice as old as that girl. The question is, how long do you have to wait before you and the little girl are the same age?"

It confused Lou, and it confused me, because the logic is mind-boggling.

After having made a filmic mess of the Army, the boys took on the Navy as their next target. In *In the Navy* they had the benefit of the Andrews Sisters again and the considerable talents of Dick Powell as a singing leading man. More classic routines, more engaging songs, and the pattern for success was pretty well established for the next decade or so. As the years rolled by, they delivered their well-aimed barbs in every conceivable format. In *Hold That Ghost*, with Joan Davis as helpmate, they found themselves in a supposedly haunted house where gangsters had hidden some loot; *Keep 'Em Flying* had Martha Raye playing a dual role to confuse Lou, and William Gargan and Dick Foran to verbally fight each other; *Ride 'Em, Cowboy* found the boys out West confusing Dick Foran and cowboy hero Johnny Mack Brown, as well as featuring Ella Fitzgerald singing "A Tisket, A Tasket, I Lost My Yellow Basket" (and the beautiful musical standard, "I'll Remember April," sung by Foran and introduced in a picturesque sequence that is usually the first thing cut out by television stations when they trim the film to fit short time slots); *Pardon My Sarong*, with Robert Paige, featuring the Ink Spots singing "If I Didn't Care," and pitting the boys against the South Sea villainy of Lionel Atwill; *Who Done It?*, a first-rate mystery-comedy that kept you guessing right to the last reel; *The Naughty Nineties*, in which the boys delivered the classic "Who's on first?" routine, and more than twenty-five other film triumphs.

Occasionally Universal Pictures, which had turned out the majority of the Abbott and Costello films, would try to turn Lou into more of a pathos-imbued foil than slapstick comedian in efforts like *It Ain't Hay*, where he accidentally causes the death of a pet horse, *Little Giant*, where he was a salesman put upon continually by an avaricious Abbott, playing a dual role, and *The Time of Their Lives*, in which Lou was a revolutionary Casper Milquetoast falsely accused of being a traitor and who comes back as a ghost in modern times to try to clear his tarnished name. These divertissements never really seemed to pay off. Audiences wanted to laugh at the boys, and the situations in these films did not present enough opportunities for general hilarity. From time to time the two comedians would leave Universal to do duty at MGM or independent studios. These efforts were similarly disappointing,

and there is little people remember from films like *Rio Rita, Lost in a Harem, Abbott and Costello in Hollywood, Africa Screams,* and *Jack and the Beanstalk* with, possibly, the sole exception of the "Slowly I turned" routine (featured in *Harem*).

In 1948 the boys went off on a new kick. Until this time, Universal's stable of captivatingly grotesque monsters (Frankenstein, Dracula, and the Wolf Man) had been relatively sacrosanct. Now the studio decided to have fun with their freakish friends and put Bud and Lou into *Abbott and Costello Meet Frankenstein*. The film was not only an exceedingly hilarious comedy, but a very good horror film to boot. It abounded with all the regular fright-film paraphernalia: misty marshes, a fog-shrouded, island-isolated castle, the standard laboratory replete with all the flashing lights and electrically discharging devices, and an all-star cast featuring Lon Chaney, Jr., as his furry-faced specialty, the Wolf Man, Bela Lugosi as a rather pasty-looking Count Dracula and Glenn Strange as the Frankenstein Monster. The film was full of entertaining little bits of business (such as the Frankenstein Monster recoiling in fear upon seeing a hypnotized Costello), cleverly written sight gags and lines. The one that never fails to break me up is delivered by Lon Chaney, Jr., to Lou over the phone. Chaney is inquiring if Lou, who plays a baggage clerk, has received two large boxes containing the supposed remains of the Frankenstein Monster and Dracula. Lou asks him simply if he has the numbers of the baggage checks, to which Chaney replies, "Never mind that. Tonight the moon will be *full!*" As though that would have *any* meaning at all to a straight-faced Lou Costello.

The pair, as well as the studio, was pleased with the results of that horror-comedy classic and they began to visit the other friendly inhabitants of the Universal crypts in *Abbott and Costello Meet the Invisible Man* and *Abbott and Costello Meet the Mummy*. Neither film even remotely approached the success of their first effort. They were slightly more successful when they appeared with that master of menace, Boris Karloff, in *Abbott and Costello Meet the Killer, Boris Karloff,* and *Abbott and Costello Meet Dr. Jekyll and Mr. Hyde*, although the success was due more to Karloff's work than their own.

Time was taking its toll on the two, however. Abbott was putting on weight, Lou was getting sluggish, and the scripts were becoming increasingly unfunny. The boys had a bad habit of repeating their favorite bits over and over in different films, and then repeating them over again on their live television shows and in their own half-hour filmed television series. People were just becoming oversaturated with Abbott and Costello. Add to those problems the fact that Abbott didn't like to work as often as he had in the past, and that Lou's frequent illnesses were drastically curtailing his effectiveness, and you had the classic picture of two giants risen to the top only to find that the only road left was downhill. Bud and Lou finally called it quits in 1956 after *Dance With Me, Henry* and went their separate ways.

Lou tried to make it on his own as a serious actor and made one feature, *The 30-Foot Bride of Candy Rock*, which was pretty awful, and a couple of television shows (a *General Electric Theater* half-hour and a *Wagon Train* drama). The rotund star who had pleased so many millions during the forties died on March 4, 1959, leaving a legacy of laughter in his films for all of us to continue to share.

Bud Abbott also ran into personal problems which almost threatened to overwhelm him. Before Lou died, Bud was in the process of suing his former partner to obtain money he maintained was due him from the team's television series. On top of that, the Government stepped in and slapped him with a tax-arrears suit that reduced the comic to pleading to all his fans who had enjoyed the team's work in the forties each to send him a dollar to help take care of the debt. Fortunately, he was able to solve his problems and is now retired, contentedly, in California.

The only other comedy team even to make a dent in Abbott and Costello's popularity was that of Dean Martin and Jerry Lewis in the fifties, but their appeal was of considerably shorter duration. Bud and Lou had the luxury, unlike Laurel and Hardy, of enjoying their success and popularity while they were making their films, and we had the good fortune to share their success with them.

Above: Nat Pendleton instructs Bud Abbott to drill Lou Costello and the other men in one of the most famous routines from *Buck Privates* (Universal 1941).

Below: Bud Abbott and Lou Costello meet The Andrew Sisters for the first time on the screen in *Buck Privates.* (Universal 1941).

Right: Lou Costello and Bud Abbott were a couple of Navy misfits in *In the Navy* (Universal 1941). *Below:* Johnny Mack Brown offers Lou Costello and Bud Abbott a job on the ranch, little realizing that they will do more harm than good in *Ride 'Em, Cowboy* (Universal 1942).

Above: Some studio aerial hi-jinks with Bud Abbott and
Lou Costello in *Keep 'Em Flying* (Universal 1941). *Below*:
Wacky fun in an amusement park involving Lou Costello
and his furry friend was a highlight of *Keep 'Em Flying*
(Universal 1941). Serial fans will recognize the fake gorilla as
the one called Satan in *Perils of Nyoka* (Republic 1942).
Right: Lou Costello demonstrates to Martha Raye how a
torpedo works by accidentally pulling the firing pin,
which, of course, leads him into a wild chase sequence in
Keep 'Em Flying (Universal 1941).

Above: Who Done It? (Universal 1942) was an excellent mystery starring the team. In this scene are Patric Knowles, Lou Costello, Bud Abbott, Ludwig Stossel, and Jerome Cowan. *Left:* A little posed horseplay with Lou Costello, Nan Wynn, and Bud Abbott in this publicity scene for *Pardon My Sarong* (Universal 1942).

Bud Abbott and Lou Costello were crowned at a special dinner at the Waldorf Astoria in New York when they were "Box Office Team Number One" in a popularity poll.

Top, left: A gagged-up publicity pose with Bud Abbott and Lou Costello for *In Society* (Universal 1944). *Top, right:* Director Charles Barton gives Lou Costello and co-star Marjorie Reynolds some suggestions on the set of *The Time of Their Lives* (Universal 1946). *Left:* A publicity photo from one of the team's MGM films, *Lost in a Harem* (MGM 1944). In this scene are Jimmy Dorsey, Marilyn Maxwell, John Conte, Bud Abbott, and Lou Costello.

Left: The boys did their famous "Who's on first?" routine in *The Naughty Nineties* (Universal 1945). This was their most popular routine, and they did it thousands of times through the years.
Below: Bud Abbott indulges Lou Costello while Patsy O'Connor watches in *It Ain't Hay* (Universal 1943).

Above: Lou Costello would like to get out of the path of a very unfriendly bull in *Mexican Hayride* (Universal 1948), but Bud Abbott stops him with, "Do you want all these people to think *I'm* a coward?" *Opposite page, bottom:* One of the team's funniest films was *Abbott and Costello Meet Frankenstein* (Universal 1948) with Bela Lugosi as Dracula and Glenn Strange as the Frankenstein Monster.

In another journey away from Universal the boys
starred in an unfunny opus titled
Africa Screams (United Artists 1949).

Top: Lon Chaney, Jr., as the Wolf Man doesn't really seem to bother Lou Costello too much in *Abbott and Costello Meet Frankenstein* (Universal 1948), but the audiences were howling. *Left*: In *Abbott and Costello Meet the Invisible Man* (Universal 1951) the team got involved with an invisible boxer who encouraged Lou to fight with his unseen assistance. *Below*: Lou Costello had a lot of laughs and thrills with Boris Karloff in *Abbott and Costello Meet the Killer, Boris Karloff* (Universal 1949).

By the time Lou Costello and Bud Abbott made *Abbott and Costello Meet the Mummy* (Universal 1955), the team had pretty well reached the end of the comedy trail.

Sabu managed to get to *the* drum in time to warn his friends of a
planned massacre in *Drums* (Korda-United Artists 1938).

3.
Bring Them Back Again
...and Again

One studio called them "Masterpiece Reprints," another "Encore Triumphs," and a third "Classic Re-Presentations." The meaning was the same—old films were coming off the racks and brought back to theaters to garner new audiences and new revenue. During the early forties hundreds of these treasures from the past were presented in local rerun houses, but there were ten films that came back so often (and I saw them *every* time they came back) that they overshadowed all the others. Most of the ten were produced by Alexander Korda in England. As far as I was concerned, and as a reflection of my personal taste, they were all action and adventure classics.

The two films which seemed to pop up endlessly and which I probably saw more than any others in this rerun derby were *Four Feathers* and *Drums* (the original English film title was *The Drum*, but we Americans like more of everything). Both films featured high English adventure in the glorious "For King and Country" tradition. *Four Feathers* was the famous tale of an officer (John Clements) who refused to leave with his regiment on the eve of battle and received a white feather, the traditional symbol of cowardice, from each of his three close comrades and a fourth from his fiancée. In order to make each take his feather back, he performs several extraordinary feats of unquestioned personal bravery. The film was full of lavish color sequences, spectacular battle scenes, and superb performances, especially that of Ralph Richardson who becomes blind from exposure to the sun and is led to safety by Clements (a secret he does not

discover until a most poignant scene at the end of the film in which, now completely and permanently blind, he feels his white feather in a small wallet left by what he thought was a native). And, of course, we mustn't forget the unforgettable scene-stealing performance by that grand old character actor C. Aubrey Smith, in which he recounts the glorious battle-filled days of his youth ("War was *war* in my day, sir!").

Drums was not quite as spectacular as an overall film but still served up a generous portion of excitement and gloriously colorful thrills. The simple plot found Raymond Massey trying to overthrow British rule in India by inviting Roger Livesey and his men to a sumptuous feast where he hoped to massacre them all. Sabu, as a young Prince befriended by Livesey, manages to get to the drum of the film's title and beat out a special predetermined coded message which Livesey recognizes. The effect of the planned attack is softened, and Massey is quickly dispatched. The excellent use of English Technicolor was never more in evidence than in this film full of dashing regimental raiments, exquisitely designed interior settings and scenic splendor.

An American double-bill that never failed to attract capacity crowds was RKO-Radio Pictures' *King Kong* and *Gunga Din*. Although hundreds of "creature" and "pseudo-Kong" films have appeared over the years, none has equalled the particular magic inherent in the original 1933 presentation. The tale of the giant ape transported from his primeval home on Skull Island to New York for exhibition purposes has enthralled several generations of thrill-seeking fans. Fay Wray screamed her way into immortality as the female lead, and Robert Armstrong's Carl Denham was a masterful characterization. The special effects, created by Willis O'Brien at a time when such things were still generally untried and unproved, have seldom until recently even been approached in their creative ingenuity.

Gunga Din is regarded by a great many people as one of the most entertaining and exciting films ever made. Filled with battle sequences spectacular enough to satisfy even the most jaded viewer, the film derives its main virtues from the interplay, physically and verbally, of its three main leads, Cary Grant, Victor McLaglen, and Douglas Fairbanks, Jr. Never was acting chemistry so right with each star filling his role with a gusto and enthusiasm instantly infectious to anyone in the audience caught up in the rhythm of the film. There is one scene in which McLaglen, after having tricked Fairbanks into signing up for a new hitch in the service, flashes an ear-to-ear smile which alone is worth the price of admission. Sam Jaffe's title-role performance as the water boy turned hero is one of finely honed perfection, as is that of Eduardo Ciannelli as the fanatical guru who exhorts his followers to "Rise and kill! Kill lest you be killed yourselves! Kill for the love of killing! Kill for the love of Kali! Kill! Kill! KILL!" And for a touching finale, Montagu Love's reading of Kipling's poem over the body of the slain Din usually had most of us shedding sympathetic tears. (Come to think of it, emotional youth that I was, I'm sure a lump came to my throat also when Kong was shot by the planes off the Empire State Building.) A major source of irritation to *Kong* and *Din* lovers was that on each reissue of the two films more and more footage was edited out to please greedy exhibitors who wanted to squeeze in additional showings. Sometimes the cuts are obvious (as, for example, the delightful scene where McLaglen dips his hands in the punch-bowl at the dance in *Din*), but many others were more subtly handled. A few frames here, a close-up there, and before you knew it many minutes from two film classics had disappeared, never again to reappear. Unfortunately, it is these truncated versions that appear on television and in theatrical reissue prints even today.

Another entertaining double-bill from RKO was *She* and *The Last Days of Pompeii*. Though not at the same classic level as *Kong* and *Din*, both films still possessed enough escapist thrills

and action to satisfy the vicarious pleasure of younger audiences. In *She* Randolph Scott, Nigel Bruce, and Helen Mack journey to a hidden city in search of a secret force that will prolong life eternally. Facing many perils, including a spectacular ice avalanche, they finally arrive at their destination and meet She-Who-Must-Be-Obeyed (Helen Gahagan), an apparently ageless beauty who has bathed in the mystical Flame of Life and thus gained immortality. Falling immediately in love with Scott, who bore a striking resemblance to a centuries-old ancestor She had killed, Gahagan plots to sacrifice Helen Mack and have Scott enter the Flame of Life and thus share eternity with her. He naturally refuses and rescues Mack just as she is about to be plunged into a sacrificial fiery pit. Gahagan, in order to demonstrate how much she has to offer compared to Mack, once again steps into the flame, but this time finds only death as she crumbles to dust before the amazed eyes of the young lovers. The most outstanding attributes of the film were the enormous eye-dazzling sets and a stirring musical score by Max Steiner (who had also composed the memorable *Kong* music).

The Last Days of Pompeii found Preston Foster rising from humble merchant to supreme gladiator and eventual pseudo-nobleman in the days of early Roman glory. His world crumbles quickly when his son decides upon Christianity and winds up as lion-fodder in the arena. In the film's rousing finale Vesuvius erupts and the city of Pompeii is completely destroyed, but not before Preston heroically dies after allowing his son to escape the clutches of villainous Louis Calhern and flee in the one boat that has escaped destruction.

Another famous Korda package was *Things to Come* (the English title was *The Shape of Things to Come*) and *The Man Who Could Work Miracles*. The latter film was a clever little minor classic which found the gods granting Roland Young, a bumbling little commonplace sort of fellow, the power to perform miracles as a test to judge man's ability to exercise restraint and good judgment. Needless to say, after Young discovers his magical power and performs some elementary feats of magic, his judgment does go awry and he winds up by stopping the sun from setting by causing the earth to cease rotating—which virtually destroys the planet by thrusting everything into space because of the interrupted momentum. As Young himself flies into space he asks that things be as they were before he obtained his miraculous power. This final request is granted, and he and earth return to their drab routine of merely existing.

Things To Come was a marvelously conceived tale of fantasy starring Raymond Massey and Ralph Richardson. The world enters a period of countless wars and is finally nearly totally devastated with only scattered tribes of people surviving. The years pass, and Massey arrives as an emissary from a modernistic city of the future to stun and amaze Richardson (playing a ruthless dictator) and his people who resemble destitute animals more than human beings. Massey, unable to convince them he is friendly, finally has to resort to sending for a squadron of planes which drop bombs filled with a harmless sleeping gas which immobilizes the populace (unfortunately, the whole affair is too much for Richardson, who apparently dies of a heart attack). Back at the modernistic city, a triumph of screen scenic design, a project is under way to send volunteers into space via means of a gigantic space gun. Sir Cedric Hardwicke, as the loyal but misguided opposition, cries out that progress has gone too far. He gathers a huge mob, who march on the gun hoping to destroy it. They are too late; the massive vehicle fires the projectile with its human inhabitants into space, and progress continues to march on.

The two final Korda extravaganzas were sometimes reissued together and, at other times, presented with an assortment of co-features. *Jungle Book* was a colorful picturization of the Kipling tales, and Sabu's performance was probably his most noteworthy. Unlike the other Korda films, *Jungle Book* was filmed entirely in the United States, and most of the film contains sumptuous interior and exterior sets. Filmed in Technicolor, the finale, a spectacularly staged forest fire, is one of the most beautiful sequences ever presented on film. The simple tale of a small boy left in the jungle and raised by wolves, then returned to civilization (which he rejects in favor of returning to his jungle paradise at the film's fadeout) has enthralled children of all ages for almost thirty years.

And last, but certainly by no means least, is my favorite fantasy film of all time, *The Thief of Bagdad*. Easily the most striking film ever done in Technicolor in the opinion of most viewers (Academy Awards went to George Perrinal for his color cinematography, to Vincent Korda for his color art direction, and to Lawrence Butler and Jack Whitney for their special effects), *The Thief of Bagdad* had all the ingredients necessary to provide audiences with unsurpassed excitement and spectacle. The villain of the piece was Conrad Veidt in the role most people remember him for, Jaffar the Magician. No villain ever presented was quite so deliciously evil. John Justin and June Duprez as the young lovers were perfect joys to watch as performers, and Rex Ingram as the Genie left nothing to be desired. The film contained so many pleasurable moments that space does not permit listing them all, but attention should be given to the sequence in which Sabu enters the temple to steal the all-seeing eye of the idol—he climbs to the top via a giant spiderweb and en route does battle with a monstrous spider; and of course the scene where Jaffar tries to escape via a mechanical horse, but is slain by an arrow fired by Sabu. Other pictorial images that remain in the memory are Jaffar, arms outstretched, calling upon his powers to create a giant storm at sea; Sabu when he first frees the Genie from his tiny bottle prison and watches him grow to gigantic proportions; the death of the Sultan by a Jaffar-bewitched statue and the simple beauty of June Duprez in a colorful garden set. If film is indeed an art, then surely *The Thief of Bagdad* must rank as the Rembrandt of film spectacle. Its color, excitement, and overall beauty have never been, nor will very likely ever be, equalled.

Of course, there were other major releases like *Lost Horizon* and *The Count of Monte Cristo*, which played from time to time. I saw them all, but the ten films I've talked about here had a special magical attraction which brought me back to the theater to see them again and again and again. And I *still* see them again and again and again, whenever the opportunity presents itself.

Opposite page, top: In *Four Feathers* (Korda-United Artists 1939)
John Clements redeems one of the symbols of cowardice by pretending
to be a mute native and leading a blinded Ralph Richardson
back to safety after a spectacular battle sequence. *Opposite page,
bottom*: One of the epic battle sequences from *Four Feathers* (Korda-
United Artists 1939). *Below*: Raymond Massey as the treacherous
Prince Ghul invites Roger Livesey, *left*, and Archibald Batty
to a dinner where he plans to massacre them and their men in
Drums (Korda-United Artists 1938).

Preston Foster was the gladiator turned
noble who rejected his beliefs when
he found his son in the arena about to be
slaughtered in *The Last Days of Pompeii*
(RKO 1935).

Right: The sacrificial procession in *She* (RKO 1935). Gustav von Seyffertitz is leading the parade and Helen Mack is under that white veil. *Below:* Helen Gahagan is in front of the elaborate throne with Randolph Scott and Nigel Bruce standing on the right as another part of the sacrificial ceremony takes place in *She* (RKO 1935).

Above: One of the intricate miniatures in *Things to Come* (Korda-United Artists 1936); the angry mobs attack the Space Gun.
Below: One of the elaborately decorated and designed sets for *Things to Come* (Korda-United Artists 1936). Raymond Massey, dressed in white, was one of the leaders in this futuristic paradise. *Opposite page:* Raymond Massey as the mysterious visitor who startles a depraved contingent of survivors of a destructive world war in *Things to Come* (Korda-United Artists 1936).

One of the amazing special-effects-created battle scenes in *King Kong*
(RKO 1933). That's heroine Fay Wray up there watching her
protector do battle.

The spectacular final sequence, touched up a little by studio still artists,
in *King Kong* (RKO 1933).

Above: Sabu challenges the authority of the watchguard serpent
guarding a fabulous treasure who seems to be bothering
young Patricia O'Rourke in *Jungle Book* (United Artists 1942).
Bottom, left: Technicians lining up a shot for a sequence
in *Jungle Book* (United Artists 1942). *Bottom, right:* Sabu
goes to buy a knife and is threatened by Joseph Calleia in
Jungle Book (United Artists 1942).

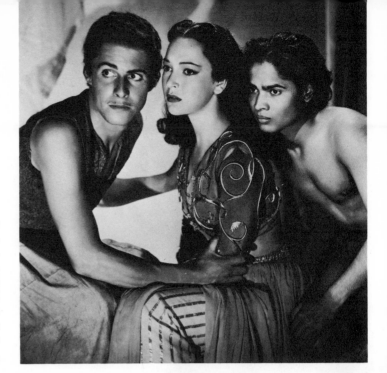

Top: John Justin, June Duprez, and Sabu were the stars of the beautifully photographed spectacle, *The Thief of Bagdad* (Korda-United Artists 1940). *Center:* Rex Ingram played the role of the Genie, seen here resting on an intricately conceived miniature, in *The Thief of Bagdad* (Korda-United Artists 1940). *Bottom:* Roland Young demonstrates his newly acquired magical powers with a simple trick to please Sophie Stewart in *The Man Who Could Work Miracles* (Korda-United Artists 1937).

Opposite page, top: Victor McLaglen engages in some verbal nonsense with
Cary Grant, not realizing he has been brutally beaten by his captors,
while Sam Jaffe, in the title role, helps to release him in *Gunga Din* (RKO
1939). *Opposite page, bottom:* Cary Grant, Victor McLaglen, and
Douglas Fairbanks, Jr., lead the spectacular charge over the rooftops of a
native village in one of the best sequences from the action-packed
Gunga Din (RKO 1939). *Below:* Eduardo Ciannelli as the fanatical Guru
taunts Victor McLaglen and Douglas Fairbanks, Jr., in
Gunga Din (RKO 1939).

When Lon Chaney, Jr., came towards the camera in close-ups like this
from *The Mummy's Tomb* (Universal 1942), most of us
hid under our seats.

4.
And Things That Go Bump in the Night

Can you remember those scenes from the movies of your youth that had you just about hiding under your theater seats, cringing in sheer terror? There are several that I can recall quite vividly. My first memory of fear goes back to the day I saw the evil Queen-turned-Witch in *Snow White and the Seven Dwarfs*. I am sure Walt Disney never intended to terrify the youthful audiences viewing the full-length animated masterpiece, but when that old hag cackled at me in giant close-up from the screen, I am sure my heart dropped clear to my feet. Of course, I was still very young when I saw that film in the late thirties, but even several years later, seeing it in reissue, I was still petrified at the sight. Another scene that absolutely scared the daylights out of me·was the classic swimming pool sequence in *Cat People*, that eerie psychological thriller turned out by Val Lewton through RKO in 1942. Jane Randolph, star Simone Simon's rival for the affections of Kent Smith, goes to a deserted swimming pool in a hotel basement. There we find her alone in the dimly illuminated room, with menacing shadows cast on the walls from light reflecting off the water in the pool. We hear the hollow echo of the water slapping against the sides of the pool, and then . . . the menacing purring of a cat! Is it Simon or the escaped black panther we saw gain his freedom earlier in the film? I wasn't sure of anything except that my knees were knocking together. And, finally, there were those damn Mummy films from Universal. I could take most of the creatures they threw at me on the screen. The Frankenstein Monster,

Dracula, the Wolf Man, the Creeper and all the others entertained but hardly frightened me. But when Tom Tyler (as the Mummy in *The Mummy's Hand*) or Lon Chaney, Jr. (as the Mummy in the three remaining films in the series) came at me on the screen with gnarled hand outstretched and the pulse-quickening music of Hans Salter gathering momentum on the soundtrack, that was just too much. I am sure there were other moments of terror that had me running home by the shortest route, but those three sequences to me were the pinnacle of moviegoing horror and suspense.

Almost all the studios tried their hands at turning out some horror material. Republic, whose basic product was Westerns, serials, and short-action programmers, had three pretty good ones that I can readily recall. *Catman of Paris* featured Carl Esmond and Adele Mara in a tale dealing with a strange kind of reincarnation; *The Lady and the Monster* was the first screen version of *Donovan's Brain* and starred Erich von Stroheim as the doctor who inveigles his assistant, Richard Arlen, to help him keep alive the brain of a rich financier who has died in an airplane crash —an act that has terrifying consequences as the brain begins to control Arlen's willpower; *Valley of the Zombies* had Robert Livingston combating Ian Keith, who had apparently become the victim of a strange living-death that could only be continued by drinking blood. All three films were very well done and one might have wished that Republic would have turned out a few more of the bloodcurdlers.

45

The other minor studios like Monogram and PRC were also turning out some scary items, such as *The Ape Man* with Bela Lugosi, *Return of the Ape Man* with Lugosi and John Carradine, *The Flying Serpent*, and *Fog Island* with George Zucco; once in a great while, the major studios would do a little dabbling in the genre themselves: MGM released *Dr. Jekyll and Mr. Hyde* with Spencer Tracy and *The Picture of Dorian Gray* with Hurd Hatfield, and Warner Bros produced *The Beast with Five Fingers*. This latter film seemed to pop up rather frequently at those great midnight Halloween shows we used to have as kids. The film has always drawn mixed reactions from viewers: some found it quite unacceptable because the audience was allowed to view what supposedly was seen only in Peter Lorre's twisted mind, while others forgot the seeming lack of logic and just relished this gory tale of a dismembered hand that supposedly went around killing people. The photography was subdued, eerie, and full of dark shadows, and Max Steiner's adaptation of music by Bach contributed to the overall mood of the picture.

RKO-Radio Pictures turned out some very interesting, as well as terrifying, horror films in addition to *Cat People*. Boris Karloff had an acting field day in such classic releases as *Isle of the Dead, The Body Snatcher*, and *Bedlam*.

But of all the studios turning out this escapist fodder, none was more profusely adept in the art as Universal Pictures. Not only did they continue to turn out features like *Frankenstein Meets the Wolf Man, House of Frankenstein, House of Dracula*, and the four mummy films, but they also kept in circulation all the great horror classics they had turned out in the thirties like the original *Frankenstein* and *Dracula*, not to mention all the sons and brides and other assorted relatives descended from them. Of all the exciting thrillers that Universal turned out, my personal favorite was the 1943 version of *The Phantom of the Opera*. The film, a remake of the silent Lon Chaney, Sr., classic, really resembled that earlier version very little. Whereas the silent film had great moments of sheer horror, this rehashing of the tale had very little in it to really frighten us except for the very brief unmasking scene at the picture's conclusion. Starring Nelson Eddy, Susanna Foster, and Claude Rains, this version was more a feast for the eye and ear than anything else. Photographed in magnificent Technicolor (it won Academy Awards for color cinematography, color art direction, and

interior color decoration), the film included among its other assets beautifully staged operatic sequences (albeit rearranged to suit script demands), enormous sets (especially the underground catacombs and lakes), and excellent performances by its stars, Eddy, Foster, Rains, Edgar Barrier and a plethora of excellent supporting players. Rains's portrayal of the opera violinist who believes his concerto has been stolen and kills the imagined thief, only to be rewarded by having a tray of etching acid thrown into his face, is certainly among his very best. It is only at very rare moments that we feel anything but the very deepest kind of pity for the pathetic man. The film was so popular that the studio seemed always to keep it in circulation via the reissue route, usually paired with another of their great color successes, *Ali Baba and the Forty Thieves*.

Another popular favorite released by Universal in 1943 was *Frankenstein Meets the Wolf Man*. This film, the fifth to feature the Frankenstein Monster and the second to utilize the hairy terror, was great escapist fun which found Lon Chaney, Jr., trying to locate Dr. Frankenstein's notebooks containing the "secrets of life and death." Along the way he met Maria Ouspenskaya in her gypsy garb, lovely Ilona Massey, and Patric Knowles, who hoped to destroy the curse that plagued Chaney every time the moon was full. Under the ruins of the house where the monster supposedly had been destroyed in a raging fire (in *Ghost of Frankenstein* one year earlier), Chaney as Larry Talbot now finds the creature safely frozen in ice. He frees him in hopes that the creature will lead him to the hidden papers. Unfortunately, the creature strikes out and we have to wait for Ilona to get the papers a few reels later. At the end of the film Knowles brings the monster back to full power, Chaney turns into his fuzzy alter-ego, and the two creatures battle each other in a fierce free-for-all that is ultimately decided when a town nut blows up a dam, sending tons of water cascading down the mountainside to inundate the deadly combatants. Fortunately, Ilona and Knowles escape to safety just in time. Chaney's transformation scenes were meticulously done (much more so than in the original *Wolf Man* film), and the film's only sour note was Bela Lugosi as the Frankenstein Monster. He simply looked terrible in the make-up.

In amongst all this superior horror fare turned out by Universal there was one little cheaply-produced PRC release I found entertaining in

1944. Called *The Monster Maker*, the film starred those two grand old acting pros, J. Carrol Naish and Ralph Morgan. Naish, playing a doctor who was experimenting with drugs to cure acromegaly, a serious disorder that causes permanent enlargement of the bones of the head, hands, and feet, injects a drug into the unsuspecting Morgan that produces the symptoms. As the film progresses, Morgan becomes more and more horribly disfigured until the final deadly confrontation in which Naish is destroyed. In the fifties Universal made a film called *Tarantula* starring Leo G. Carroll that also utilized acromegaly as source material.

After all these years, do those classic horror films hold up? A lot depends upon your point of view. They are certainly popular television fare, with almost every city running its own particular type of *Creature Feature* film festival featuring all the old Universal stand-bys. But there is a marked difference: these films were made to be seen in darkened theaters, uninterrupted and uncut. After all, how can you be really frightened by these films when you're sitting in the comfort of a warmly lit living room with parents or friends keeping noisy company with you? No, I think the only way you can recapture the real spirit of these productions is to view them in their original habitats. Even then, in a world full of real-life suffering and horror, I don't quite think that the Wolf Man, Count Dracula, the Frankenstein Monster, the Mummy and all the other delightful monstrosities that peopled those tiny screens in thousands of theaters decades ago carry very much weight anymore. We have matured just too much.

She was one of the dreaded "Cat People"—doomed to slink and prowl by night . . . fearing always that a lover's kiss might change her into a snarling, clawing KILLER!

CAT PEOPLE

DON'T BE SURPRISED AT ANYTHING YOU SEE!!!

with

SIMONE SIMON

KENT SMITH • TOM CONWAY

JANE RANDOLPH • JACK HOLT

Re-release by R K O RADIO PICTURES

Produced by VAL LEWTON • Directed by JACQUES TOURNEUR
Written by DeWitt Bodeen

J. Carrol Naish turned Ralph Morgan into this grotesque creature in *The Monster Maker* (PRC 1944).

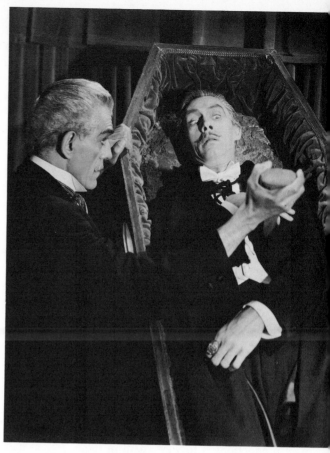

Above: Boris Karloff, who had removed a stake from a skeleton of Dracula and saw John Carradine materialize as the bloodsucker, now threatens to replace it unless he gets a little cooperation in *House of Frankenstein* (Universal 1945).
Opposite page: Claude Rains leads Susanna Foster to his hideaway in the catacombs under the Paris Opera House in *The Phantom of the Opera* (Universal 1943).

Right: When opera officials fail to heed his repeated warnings, Claude Rains as the horribly disfigured Phantom cuts down the massive chandelier over the heads of a packed audience in *The Phantom of the Opera* (Universal 1943). *Above:* Peter Lorre feels the deadly pressure of Victor Francen's piano-playing hand on his throat in *The Beast with Five Fingers* (Warner Bros 1946). Supposedly it was this same dismembered hand that went crawling around killing assorted victims.

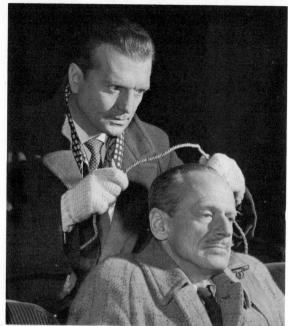

Top, left: A mysterious killer strikes a small town, and the people believe his handiwork to be that of an escaped cat. Margo is the victim in this scene from *The Leopard Man* (RKO 1943). *Top, right:* John Loder was *The Brighton Strangler* (RKO 1945) who dreamed he went about murdering people like Miles Mander in this publicity pose.
Bottom: Una O'Connor doesn't quite know what to make of Claude Rains's bandaged face in *The Invisible Man* (Universal 1933).

Above: Boris Karloff and Bela Lugosi have some interesting plans for poor Samuel S. Hinds in *The Raven* (Universal 1935). *Right:* The ever popular Vera Hruba Ralston and Richard Arlen fell under the scientific spell of Erich von Stroheim in *The Lady and the Monster* (Republic 1944), the first film version of *Donovan's Brain*.

Rondo Hatton played the Creeper in several films, including *House of Horrors* (Universal 1946).

Boris Karloff in his most famous role as the Frankenstein Monster in *Frankenstein* (Universal 1931).

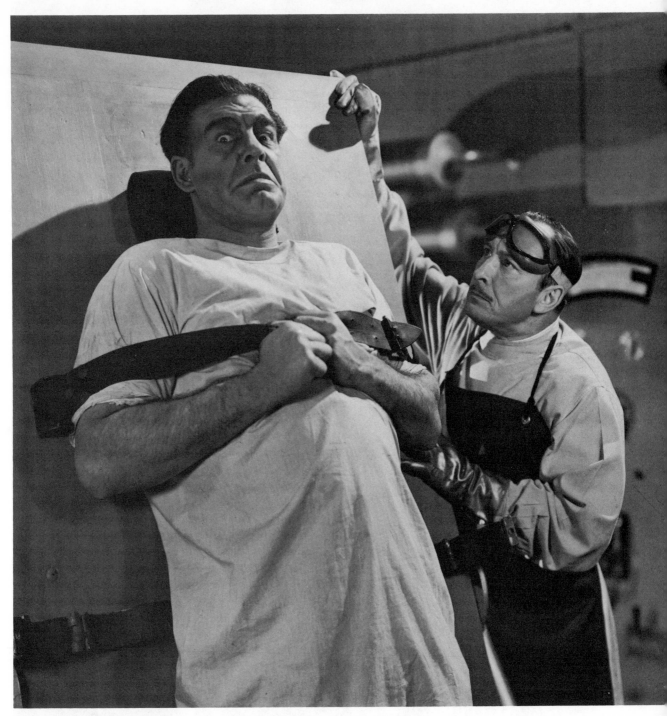

Opposite page, bottom: Karloff and Lugosi had the benefit
of Henry Daniell's assistance in *The Body Snatcher*
(RKO 1945). *Above:* Lionel Atwill was the scientist
who turned Lon Chaney, Jr., into a *Man-Made Monster*
(Universal 1941). *Opposite page, top:* Colin Clive, *left,*
and Ernest Thesiger watch as their newest creation,
played by Elsa Lanchester, makes her debut in *The Bride of
Frankenstein* (Universal 1935), which many people
believe to be the best film in the series.

Red Skelton gave Ann Sothern a helping, though apparently missing, hand in this scene from *Maisie Gets Her Man* (MGM 1942), one in a series of excellent comedy films featuring the female cut-up.

5.
The Best Medicine

During times of great national stress, it is usually the entertainment industry that is called upon to help us maintain our sense of humor in the face of adversity. World War II was one of those periods in our history, and the motion picture industry fulfilled its role most nobly by providing us with a wonderful variety of laughter on the screen to help us forget the everyday problems of waging a war for survival. Every studio, large and small, was turning out series comedies, big-budget frolics, musicals, or all-star extravaganzas, and we all found ourselves eagerly caught up in this continuing whirlpool of rib-tickling entertainment.

Family comedies were immensely successful, and the kind you enjoyed most may have reflected your view of your own home situation. For those who believed Dad was a bungler and all-around imbecile, you had the Blondie series. Based on the popular newspaper strip, which is very likely the most widely read in comics history, Arthur Lake as Dagwood and Penny Singleton as Blondie were perfect choices to re-create the inspired lunacy of Chic Young's characters. Indeed, both of them became so identified with these roles that they found their careers as actors virtually destroyed, much the same way Basil Rathbone was type-cast as Sherlock Holmes and Ralph Byrd as Dick Tracy. Although I enjoyed both Lake and Singleton in the number of Blondie films I saw during the time (they did twenty-eight films in all from 1938 to 1951), it was the remarkable performances of Larry Simms (as Baby Dumpling) and Daisy, the dog, that never failed to amaze and delight me.

More idiocy was evident in the popular Henry Aldrich series turned out by Paramount. Jimmy Lydon as Henry and Charles Smith as Homer seemed to get into absolutely incredible situations which seemed almost impossible to resolve. In *Henry Aldrich, Editor*, for example, he ran the school paper. He met a timid little stranger at the scene of a fire who convinced Henry that he could tell the youngster about forthcoming fires in advance. Naturally our young hero started writing about the fires in advance of their happening, and soon the entire town believed he was the one who was really starting them. Before the adventure ended, Henry and his informer, who of course was the real arsonist, were almost trapped in a blazing inferno.

Ann Sothern as Maisie was also around in a number of wacky adventures that found her either helping people out of trouble, or getting into it herself. MGM produced the glossy series, and Red Skelton made an appearance in one of the early adventures. That same studio also turned out the popular Dr. Kildare programmers, which, although not basically funny in premise, did treat its problems with singular lightheartedness. And, of course, MGM also turned out the real giant of the family comedies, the Hardy family films. No matter what problems Mickey Rooney (as Andy Hardy) got into, one good long talk with Judge Hardy (beautifully played by Lewis Stone) usually set everything straight. Probably no other series in screen history so endeared itself to our World War II generation as this.

While Abbott and Costello were the undisputed champions of twin-effort comedy, there were a few other teams that managed to engender sizable laughs from time to time. Olsen and Johnson had brought their inspired zaniness to the screen in the thirties in items like *Fifty Million Frenchmen,* but it was after their record-breaking Broadway success with *Hellzapoppin* that they really captured the public's fancy. They transferred *Hellzapoppin* to the screen in 1941 and followed it with such popular hits as *Crazy House, Ghost Catchers,* and *See My Lawyer.* The films were all full of incredible sight gags, outrageous puns, and a wacky kind of undisciplined mayhem heretofore unknown to moviegoers. Olsen and Johnson would seldom enter a room through a door—they'd just blow a hole in the wall and plow right through.

Wally Brown and Alan Carney were RKO's claim to the twosome title, but I found them usually bland and unfunny. Perhaps it wasn't really their fault but the fault of the writers who were trying to build them into something they really weren't qualified to be. *Zombies on Broadway* was very likely their biggest success, but even that fails to hold up well today.

When Bing Crosby and Bob Hope teamed up it was really big-time humor. Both singer and comedian had large personal followings and had starred in numerous successful musical and comedy films on their own, but when they teamed up the result was a special kind of screen magic that was hard to top. One sure way to start an argument between film buffs is to get them to try and pick their favorite "road" picture. Many like their first efforts, *The Road to Singapore* and *The Road to Zanzibar,* done in 1940 and 1941 respectively. Few tend to like the later ones, *The Road to Bali* (the only one made in color) which appeared in 1952 or *The Road to Hong Kong,* the last of the series to date, made in 1962. It is the middle group which I find most entertaining, and my own favorite has always been *The Road to Morocco,* a 1942 entry that not only had the standard Hope-Crosby humor but also introduced one of my favorite movie songs, "Moonlight Becomes You," sung by Crosby. The other titles, for the record, were *The Road to Utopia* (1945) and *The Road to Rio* (1947).

W. C. Fields had made his most successful and popular films in the thirties for Paramount, but in the forties he turned out four films for Universal that have come to be regarded as comedy gems. *The Bank Dick* was certainly the most memorable, but *You Can't Cheat an Hon-*

est Man (in which favorite radio rivals Edgar Bergen and Charlie McCarthy played co-starring roles), *Never Give a Sucker an Even Break* and *My Little Chickadee* (with Mae West matching him laugh for laugh) were all box-office successes as well.

Because radio played such an important part in our lives in those pre-television days, it was only natural that the studios would bring a great many audio favorites to the movie screen. RKO turned out quite a few that found stars like Kay Kyser (*You'll Find Out*), the Great Gildersleeve (*Gildersleeve's Ghost*), Fibber McGee and Molly (*Heavenly Days*), and others each appearing in his own series of adventures. Sometimes they would use several together (McGee, Molly, Gildersleeve, and Edgar Bergen and Charlie McCarthy appeared jointly in films like *Look Who's Laughing* and *Here We Go Again*) for added box-office appeal. RKO also turned out the popular series of Mexican Spitfire films featuring tempestuous Lupe Valez and her ever suffering co-star, Leon Errol.

Over at Republic they were churning out a very popular series of films starring Judy Canova. Judy was a particular favorite of small-town audiences who loved the hillbilly type of humor she specialized in. Titles like *Sleepy Lagoon* and *Sis Hopkins* usually featured tales about city slickers trying to outfox the country folk but eventually being outwitted themselves. The comedienne also had a very pleasant singing voice, and her songs were always an additional bonus. My favorite film in this series was *Chatterbox* with Joe E. Brown (who was another comedy favorite in a series of Columbia films during these years) playing a radio cowboy, Rex Vane, who suddenly finds he has to prove himself in real life.

Red Skelton began his screen career in a small role in *Having Wonderful Time,* a 1938 film starring Ginger Rogers, and he went on to become a leading box-office draw for MGM in the forties. I particularly enjoyed his three-film series in which he played a radio detective called the Fox who turned his attention to solving real-life mysteries (*Whistling in the Dark, Whistling in Brooklyn,* and *Whistling in Dixie*), but I am sure most of his fans would prefer efforts like *A Southern Yankee, I Dood It* and *DuBarry Was a Lady,* as well as the long string of popular musicals he did with stars like Esther Williams.

Jack Benny turned in some funny work in films like *Charley's Aunt, George Washington Slept Here,* and *The Horn Blows at Midnight* (although Benny has kidded about how badly this film was received, it really is an enjoyable movie). Trying to keep up with Jack was his long-time friend and radio rival, Fred Allen, who had a ball doing little items like *It's in the Bag*.

There seemed to be an endless supply of unimportant musical comedies starring the Andrews Sisters, Allan Jones, Gale Storm, Jane Frazee, and others. Probably the most successful of these minor musicales were those in which Donald O'Connor and Peggy Ryan sang, danced, and mugged their way through every possible backstage plot to the obvious delight of audiences.

The list seems virtually endless as far as laughmakers were concerned, and I haven't even included all those great stars who made those delightful two-reelers that used to be a part of every Saturday matinee: men like Edgar Kennedy, Leon Errol, Andy Clyde, the Three Stooges, etc. And how about those *Pete Smith Specialties* and the popular *Speaking of Animals* series. I wonder how many people remember Lew Lahr, who used to come in for some funny bits at the end of those *Fox Movietone Newsreels* we saw every week? Remember Joe McDoakes (George O'Hanlon), popping up from behind that eight-ball in a popular series of one-reelers?

It may have seemed a frivolous luxury to sit in a theater and laugh while the world was in torment, and I am sure there are those who would say our time should have been spent elsewhere. Perhaps they are right; I don't know. I only know that it seemed right at the time, and I wish we had a little more laughter today to give us a break from the tension of the conflicts we currently face.

Right: W. C. Fields and Leon Errol were up to their usual nonsense in *Never Give a Sucker an Even Break* (Universal 1941). *Below:* Judy Canova and Joe E. Brown were hilarious in *Chatterbox* (Republic 1943), a story that found Brown playing a radio cowboy who was signed to make a real Western film.

Top: Sheldon Leonard, now a successful television producer, played his typical gangster role for the benefit of Wally Brown and Alan Carney in *Zombies on Broadway* (RKO 1945). *Center:* Edgar Bergen and his wooden pal Charlie McCarthy were only two of the radio stars who appeared in *Here We Go Again* (RKO 1942). *Bottom:* Charles Smith and Rita Quigley were almost trapped with Jimmy Lydon, *right,* as Henry in a dangerous fire in *Henry Aldrich, Editor* (Paramount 1942).

Above: Peggy Ryan and Donald O'Connor were audience favorites in a series of musicals like *Patrick the Great* (Universal 1945), from which this scene is taken. *Right:* Lupe Velez clowned with her frequent co-star, Leon Errol, in one of her popular series features, *Mexican Spitfire's Blessed Event* (RKO 1943).

Top: Among the most famous scenes on movie screens during the late thirties and early forties were Mickey Rooney's talks with Lewis Stone such as this one from *The Courtship of Andy Hardy* (MGM 1942). *Bottom:* I wonder if Anthony Quinn suspects some horseplay in this sequence from *The Road to Morocco* (Paramount 1942) with Bing Crosby and Bob Hope.

W. C. Fields was absolutely hilarious
as *The Bank Dick* (Universal 1940).

Left: Ole Olsen, *left*, and Chic Johnson do a bit of clowning with co-star Martha Raye in this publicity pose from *Hellzapoppin* (Universal 1941). *Below:* Willie Best turned in an excellent comic performance along with Bob Hope in *The Ghost Breakers* (Paramount 1940), which was remade in the fifties with Dean Martin and Jerry Lewis, renamed *Scared Stiff* (Paramount 1953).

Arthur Lake as Dagwood and Penny Singleton as Blondie frequently took
second-place acting honors to the performances of the scene-stealing Larry Simms (as
Baby Dumpling) and Daisy (the tiny dog) in films like *Blondie in Society*
(Columbia 1941), from which this scene is taken.

Harold Peary as Gildersleeve and Nicodemus seem to have discovered
Gildersleeve's Ghost (RKO 1944) in this film from the popular series
based on the radio show.

Above: Kay Kyser and his orchestra made
several popular features. In *Carolina Blues*
(Columbia 1944) he introduced lovely
Ann Miller. *Right:* The great Marx Brothers
films were made in the thirties, but films
like *The Big Store* (MGM 1941) did manage
to provide a few laughs. The boys are
surrounding Marion Martin in this
publicity pose.

Top: Shirley Temple was still captivating audiences in new films and reissues like *The Little Princess* (Twentieth Century-Fox 1939); here she is in a scene with Arthur Treacher. *Bottom:* Margaret O'Brien could melt anyone's heart, including Wallace Beery's, in films like *Bad Bascomb* (MGM 1946).

Jack Benny had a field day in the film version of *Charley's Aunt*
(Twentieth Century-Fox 1941). That's Edmund Gwenn looking over
the wall, while Richard Haydn, *left*, and James Ellison help Jack dress.

Boris Karloff played the oriental detective Mr. Wong in a popular series of mysteries for Monogram.

6.

The Fun Factory

While my moviegoing elders were extolling the virtues of such quality mystery fare as *The Maltese Falcon, The Big Sleep, Murder, My Sweet, And Then There Were None*, and *Laura*, I was jumping up and down in my matinee seat over a little Monogram cheapie called *The Mystery of the 13th Guest*. A virtual scene-for-scene remake of the 1932 *The Thirteenth Guest* starring Ginger Rogers and Lyle Talbot, this version featured Dick Purcell and Helen Parrish in what many believe is the perfect model for a Saturday afternoon thriller. The film was filled with all the gimmicks the kids loved: a mysterious masked murderer, hidden passageways, an eerie deserted mansion, an electrically wired phone to kill the victims, a motley group of suspects, and three wisecracking detectives (two police, one private). The plot found Helen Parrish returning to a deserted house on her twenty-first birthday to read a letter left by her grandfather thirteen years earlier. Inside the letter is the cryptic message "13-13-13," which turned out to be the number of a safe deposit box. She is quickly disposed of (it later turns out she was an impostor who had had plastic surgery done on her face to resemble the real heir), and more murders occur (the bodies being placed in the identical chairs, of which there were a total of, you guessed it, thirteen, in which all the relatives were seated at the dinner party when the letter was originally presented). The wisecracking private eye was played to perfection by Dick Purcell, and the bumbling police by Tim Ryan, who also had a hand in writing the screenplay, and Frank Faylen.

Two other interesting mysteries turned out by Monogram which were extremely pleasing to watch were *The Phantom Killer* (another remake), in which John Hamilton played a dual role as brothers, one of whom went around murdering people while the other established an alibi, and *The Living Ghost*, a tale that involved turning a man into a walking zombie as the result of a sinister operation. James Dunn gave an excellent performance in the latter film as a sardonic private detective assisted by one of the great ladies of B-films, Joan Woodbury.

No matter what your personal tastes may have been for B-film fodder in the forties, Monogram satisfied you by turning out something in almost every conceivable category. In the Western field they had Johnny Mack Brown, the Range Busters, the Rough Riders, Tex Ritter, and others turning out regular series every year. For action a little further north, they picked up the Renfrew of the Mounted series, which Grand National had started, and turned out some excellent little thrillers starring James Newill. For aerial entertainment, John Trent was Tailspin Tommy in several entertaining programmers. Musicals? They had an endless variety of those, with titles like *Campus Rhythm, Rhythm Parade, Spotlight Scandals*, and *Hot Rhythm*, all full of simply awful numbers filmed against the cheapest sets imaginable. For horror devotees they turned out such pleasant little diverse attractions as *The Ape*, with Boris Karloff jumping around in a furry costume, *The Ape Man* with Bela Lugosi sporting a shaggy face, *Return of the Ape Man*, which found Bela Lugosi taking John Carradine's brain and transplanting it in the head of a Neanderthal man, and *King of the Zombies* and *Revenge of the Zombies*, two grotesque little thrillers that made their black actors look so silly that I am sure we will not quickly see these films shown in public again. Boxing fans were rewarded with the Joe Palooka series, based on the famous comicstrip character, with Joe Kirkwood, Jr., as Joe and Leon Errol as his comical pal, Knobby Walsh.

But of all the material turned out by Monogram's fun factory, probably the three most entertaining and successful series were those which featured Sidney Toler (and later Roland Winters) as Charlie Chan, Kane Richmond as the Shadow, and the seemingly endless parade of East Side Kids adventures.

Although the three Shadow films were entertaining, they were far from being well-made little gems. Instead of mystery and thrills, as one would normally expect, the plots featured more comedy than anything else. Barbara Reed as Margot Lane was always getting in the way of star Kane Richmond with her silly jealous tantrums, causing a boring interruption in the action. The first film of the three, *The Shadow Returns*, was probably the best in the group, and found our hero solving a mystery in which the victims of a mysterious killer were dragged to their deaths from various balconies by means of a bullwhip. In *Behind the Mask*, the masked nemesis of crime solved the murder of a newspaper reporter who was killed in his own office by a killer whose shadow was seen on the glass door of the office but who seemed to disappear from sight almost immediately afterward. (As it turned out, the killer simply climbed out the window to a balcony and re-entered the office to join the crowd rushing to the scene of the murder.) The final effort, *The Missing Lady*, was the weakest film: the Shadow searched out a valuable art piece carved in the shape of a woman, and Miss Reed's antics in this last film were positively nerve-racking as she managed to spend almost three quarters of the film botching things up.

The single most popular mystery series turned out by Monogram was, of course, the Charlie Chan films. Twentieth Century-Fox had thrown in the towel on production of the celebrated detective's exploits in 1942, after having made twenty-eight films starring first Warner Oland and then Sidney Toler. Monogram brought Toler back to do eleven new films beginning in 1944

and wound up their Chan endeavors with six films made in 1947–49 starring Roland Winters after Toler's death. Again, as in the case of the Shadow films, humor was overstressed in the films to the detriment of the action. Admittedly, Mantan Moreland as the comedy relief was infinitely more tolerable to take than Barbara Reed (as a matter of fact, it was Mantan's work that added so much to the general appeal of this particular series), but one might have wished for a little more mystery and a little less nonsense. The Monogram efforts tended to be filled with a great deal more gimmickery than the Fox films: one was amazed at the seemingly infinite variety of fascinating ways to kill people. Probably the most elaborate device was in *The Scarlet Clue*. The killer, wearing a grotesque theatrical mask, sends his intended victims a teletype message instructing them to go to a certain floor in a specific elevator, look out to see if anyone is there and, if not, to go to a higher floor. As the victim reaches his first stop to make his initial observation we see the mysterious killer peeking through a crack in a partially opened door and then pulling an electrical switch. The doors to the elevator close and it starts its ascent, when suddenly the bottom swings open like a trap door and the victim plunges to his death. Great gory fun, of course, but somehow I am sure most of us wondered how such an involved death trap could ever have been installed in the first place. One film had a gun that fired with the aid of an electromagnet, and another had a weapon that fired a bullet made of ice, which of course melted, leaving another baffling challenge to be met by the Oriental sleuth. Toler, who was not Chinese, was excellent in the role of Chan, and the films usually featured an interesting assortment of capable performers as suspects.

Following close on the heels of the Chan films as far as popularity was concerned was the infinite variety of East Side Kids comedies. Although the series continued into the middle fifties (with Huntz Hall outrageously mugging and burlesquing his earlier characterization in unfunny vehicles), it is the films turned out in the early forties that most of us remember and enjoy best. The whole series, quite naturally, had exceptional appeal for children, who, for all practical purposes, saw themselves being pictured on the screen. There seemed to be no end of trouble that the Kids could get themselves into. Usually Bobby Jordan was the scapegoat who got blamed for assorted mayhem (including murder), and

Leo Gorcey, Huntz Hall, "Sunshine" Sammy Morrison (the only regular black member of the gang), and Gabriel Dell (who alternated between being a gang member and being a villain) were called upon to get him out of his current predicament. The most entertaining films in the series for most were probably those that pitted the gang against that perennial screen menace, Bela Lugosi: *Ghosts on the Loose* (which had Ava Gardner playing a small role) and *Spooks Run Wild*. Both had the youngsters running rampant through houses that were supposedly haunted, but which were really being used to cover the illicit activities (counterfeiting, for example) of Lugosi and his gang. My own favorite in the series, and the one which seemed to come back to theaters more often than most, was *Clancy Street Boys*. The plot was relatively simple: rancher Pete Monahan (excellently played by that grand old pro, Noah Beery, Sr.) and his daughter come to New York to visit Muggs (Leo Gorcey) and his mother. Before he died, Muggs's father had told the rancher that he had seven kids (six boys and one girl), and for many years Pete has been sending money to the supposed family as birthday and Christmas gifts. Muggs, in a bold move, has the gang impersonate the family with Glimpy (Huntz Hall) posing as the girl. A gangster gets wind of the scheme and threatens to expose the whole plan, but, when Muggs decides to confess the subterfuge himself, has his gang capture the wealthy rancher in order to extort money. Happily, this film ends, as almost all of them ended, with a pitched battle between the gang of kids and the gangsters.

One would never try to suggest that Monogram turned out quality product (except in rare instances when a *Suspense* or *The Hunted* might pop up), but they certainly turned out a great many films that thrilled and delighted my generation of front-row fanatics. On this score Monogram certainly ranked high, and indeed was a fun factory.

IS HE MAN or ZOMBIE? Strange secrets of a scientific killer!

"THE LIVING GHOST"

with JAMES DUNN JOAN WOODBURY

A Monogram PICTURE

Top: This was the mysterious killer in the Charlie Chan adventure *The Scarlet Clue* (Monogram 1945). *Center:* Pierre Watkin, Joseph Crehan, and Edward Gargan just think they have the Shadow trapped in *Behind the Mask* (Monogram 1946). Kane Richmond is behind the particular mask in this scene. *Bottom:* James Newill and Dave O'Brien were the stars of a number of Renfrew of the Mounted films like *Yukon Flight* (Monogram 1939).

Above: Barbara Reed, *left,* added to Kane Richmond's troubles in *Behind the Mask* (Monogram 1946). *Below:* John Carradine discovered a way to keep Veda Ann Borg, his dead wife, alive in *Revenge of the Zombies* (Monogram 1943).

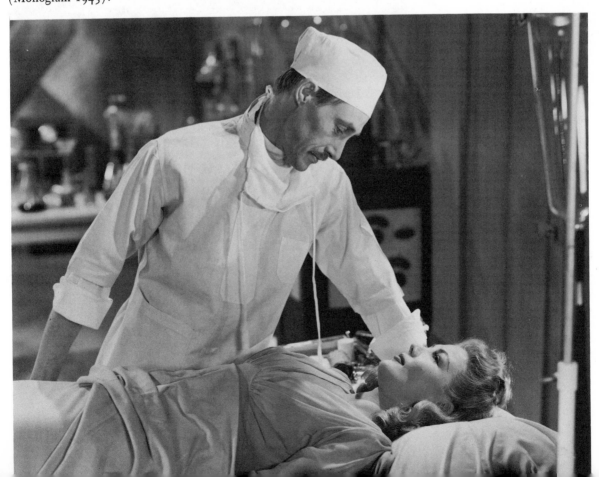

Top: Frank Faylen, Tim Ryan, and Dick Purcell believe that the mysterious killer intends to "line the table with stiffs" in *The Mystery of the 13th Guest* (Monogram 1943). *Center:* The masked killer has Helen Parrish in his clutches in *The Mystery of the 13th Guest* (Monogram 1943). *Bottom:* John Hamilton, playing a dual role, sets up an alibi with Mantan Moreland while his twin commits a murder in *Phantom Killer* (Monogram 1942).

Typical youth-oriented films like *The Gang's All Here* (Monogram 1940) with Frankie Darro, Marcia Mae Jones, Jackie Moran, Keye Luke, and Mantan Moreland were a staple of Monogram in the thirties and forties.

If Mantan Moreland looks a little silly in this scene with Sidney Toler from *The Scarlet Clue* (Monogram 1945) he has good reason: the floor of that elevator opens like a trap door and is the killer's way of eliminating his victims.

Right: Monogram turned out quite a few straight gangster yarns like *Federal Bullets* (Monogram 1937) with, *left*, Milburn Stone, (Doc of TV's *Gunsmoke*) and John Merton. *Below:* A big, lavish musical extravaganza (Monogram style) with Gale Storm, *center*, from *Rhythm Parade* (Monogram 1942).

Left: Guy Kibbee, Leon Errol (as Knobby Walsh), Elyse Knox, and Joe Kirkwood, Jr. (as Joe Palooka) in *Gentleman Joe Palooka* (Monogram 1946), one in a series of films based on the comic strip character created by Ham Fisher. *Below:* Roland Winters as Charlie Chan and Robert Livingston in *The Feathered Serpent* (Monogram 1948).

Top, left: Bobby Jordan, Leo Gorcey and Huntz Hall face another crisis in *Smart Alecks* (Monogram 1942), one of the very popular East Side Kids comedy-adventures. *Top, right:* Irene Rich and Charles Bickford were the stars of *Queen of the Yukon* (Monogram 1940), one of the studio's better outdoor action films. *Bottom:* James Dunn was almost the recipient of that knife in *The Living Ghost* (Monogram 1942). That's Joan Woodbury next to him and Gus Glassmire on the floor.

Top: Irene Ryan, *left,* and strip-tease artist Ann Corio cavorted in *The Sultan's Daughter* (Monogram 1943). Miss Ryan is much better known to today's audiences as "Granny" on TV's popular *Beverly Hillbillies,* and was married to Tim Ryan, who wrote many of the scripts for Monogram films, when they appeared as the popular comedy team of Tim and Irene. *Bottom:* Marjorie Reynolds, Milburn Stone, and John Trent were the stars of four Tailspin Tommy adventures made in 1939 by Monogram.

Tom Tyler as the costumed hero is about to unmask the mysterious Scorpion in *Adventures of Captain Marvel* (Republic 1941).

7.
Saturdays Are for Thrills

In an exhibitor's production guide (a lavishly illustrated brochure put out by the studio to announce its forthcoming product for the year) issued by Republic Pictures in 1942, the following introduction appeared before the pages devoted to new serials: "ACTION speaks louder than WORDS! Every exhibitor knows that a serial depends on its red-blooded action rather than on a barrage of 'talk-talk.' That is why the serial has endured since the inception of the industry, and no doubt it will outlast any other type of motion picture composition. In fact serials become more popular year by year with audiences. Serials must have a staff which is temperamentally suited to this action type product. The personnel must live, breathe and love their work, and they firmly believe that every serial is equally as important to audiences as *Gone with the Wind*. The outstanding success of Republic serials has been largely due to the organization of our incomparable technical staff, who apply themselves diligently and conscientiously to a job that they enjoy. Here's to Action Product! REPUBLIC STUDIOS."

While Republic may have been mistaken concerning the lasting durability of the serials, they certainly were correct, as far as I was concerned, in stressing the action elements of their product.

Oakland, California, in those days of my serial-going youth was a large enough city to have complete coverage of the chapter-plays turned out by the three producing companies. The Central Theater, primarily a rerun house, featured the Universal talk-a-thons; the Rex Theater, an abominably dilapidated scratch house which ran triple features, catered to Columbia devotees; and the Broadway Theater, my home away from home, inherited the Republic material. It had taken only a visit or two to each theater in 1940 and my mind was quickly made up. I craved action, not talk, and only the Republic product seemed to offer action in abundance. I was hooked, and for the next seven years of my life, with very few weekly exceptions, I spent every Saturday afternoon watching twenty-six consecutively produced action-packed thrillers.

I am often asked, because I write so much about Republic serials, which is my personal favorite. I find it an impossible question to answer without a considerable amount of hedging, for I quite honestly loved them all. After all, with few exceptions, they were all cast from the same mold. Each contained a plethora of fights, chases, explosions, and assorted thrills. What emerged after those seven years, then, was a kaleidoscopic tapestry woven into the fabric of my mind that contained the very best elements of all twenty-six films joined together to form, if you will, a montage that I called simply *the* Republic serial. Fortunately, beginning in 1961 I was able to once again view these films which had given me so much pleasure as a child. To my surprise and delight almost all of them were as exciting as I had remembered them to be, and I now find myself able to objectively sort them into general categories.

My favorite plot serial, for example, was *Adventures of Captain Marvel*. This exciting tale of the mysterious black-hooded Scorpion and his quest for the lenses to complete his devilish Golden Scorpion Atom Smasher was a joy to watch. This particular serial didn't have quite as much action in it, primarily due to the leading character's general invulnerability, but it made up for the deficiency by utilizing superb special effects and daredevil stunts by David Sharpe, doubling for lead Tom Tyler.

As all-around action films I would choose *The Masked Marvel* and *Secret Service in Darkest Africa*. Never were fight sequences more numerous or better staged, thanks to the directorial skill of Spencer Gordon Bennet and ace stuntmanship of Tom Steele and the Republic staff. No audience I was ever a part of in those days could ever remain seated after one of the massive set-destroying melees in these films.

My choice for favorite leading man in serials must be evenly divided between Kane Richmond and Allan Lane. Richmond was a perfect choice to play the lead in *Spy Smasher* (I really should say *leads*, because he played a dual role), Republic's smash follow-up in the comic-strip-adaptation vein a year after *Captain Marvel*. One of the best points in his favor was that he could act. This was no small feat, for the serials were full of people who *couldn't* act (look at the four leads in *The Masked Marvel*, for example). Republic brought Richmond back a couple of years later as the lead in *Haunted Harbor*, and he helped make that serial equally enjoyable, teamed up with their current serial queen, Kay Aldridge. Allan Lane was also able to lend his particular brand of he-man appeal successfully to his four serial adventures: *King of the Royal Mounted*, *King of the Mounties*, *Daredevils of the West*, and *The Tiger Woman*. After his serial chores, Lane went on to become one of Republic's most successful Western stars (billed as Allan "Rocky" Lane). Many years later, one of the worst-kept secrets in television history was that Lane did the voice for the famous talking horse, Mr. Ed, in that popular series of the early sixties.

Sometimes I enjoyed a serial simply because I remembered a single chapter ending that was so unusual, as opposed to the routine explosions and car crashes, that it remained in my memory long after I had forgotten the rest of the serial. In *G-Men vs. the Black Dragon*, an action-packed wartime epic starring Rod Cameron, there was an ingenious ending which found leading lady Constance Worth being captured by the villains and tied to a chair. Opposite the chair was a cabinet in which was placed a spear aimed directly at the helpless heroine. By the spear were two tiny Japanese figurines holding miniature spears. These figures slowly rotated towards each other and when the tips of the two spears touched the contact set the full-size missile flying directly towards the wide-eyed prisoner. And, of course, while all of this was going on a monumental fight sequence was in progress as Cameron tried to effect a rescue (which, in the next chapter, he naturally managed).

Another equally elaborate trap was laid by George J. Lewis for hero Marten Lamont in *Federal Operator 99*. Lamont, in disguise, enters an old building and moves down a passageway, at the end of which he spies Lewis sitting behind a desk. Lewis makes a sudden movement and Lamont fires a gun at him—but Lewis has erected a bulletproof glass partition in front of himself. Our hero then turns to make his escape, only to find his way blocked by a barred gate which Lewis closes at the other end of the passageway by remote control. Now completely trapped, Lamont is informed by Lewis that his imprisonment was only part of a surprise, and that now he is "going to get the rest of it." Another switch is thrown and a series of outlet pipes at the base of the passageway begin to emit huge bursts of flame. The scene fades as the jets of searing death move closer and closer to Lamont and the camera lens. How did he escape? Well, I won't hold you in suspense. His female aide, Helen Talbot, enters just in time to open the barred gate from the outside! How else?

Villainy skillfully played can be an entertaining inducement to return week after week. The top contributor in that category was Roy Barcroft. Roy managed to overshadow the acting performances of even the leading men in his two favorite serials, *Manhunt of Mystery Island* and *The Purple Monster Strikes*. In the first serial he played Captain Mephisto, a Mephistophelean character created by having one of four suspects sit in a "transformation" chair that altered his appearance to resemble an ancient piratical inhabitant of the island. There is an entertaining scene in which Barcroft explains the process to henchman Kenne Duncan. He speaks of changing the molecular structure of his body. Kenne nods a knowing smile and says, " I understand"—whereupon Barcroft smiles and counters with, "If I thought that you did, I'd kill you." In *The Purple Monster Strikes* Roy was an alien from Mars who came to Earth to steal the plans of a scientist (James Craven) for building a more powerful rocket than the Martians had been able to develop, with the eventual intention of using the new rockets for a later invasion. Roy, who usually weighed over two hundred pounds, had to slim down to a hundred and eighty to wear the tights he was required to don in the role. He often recalled how the crew used to call him "the jerk in tights from Boyle Heights" while he was making the film. He was truly a remarkable villain, with a real-life heart of gold.

The leading lady in the last two serials mentioned (as well as four others: *The Tiger Woman*, *Zorro's Black Whip*, *The Crimson Ghost*, and *Jesse James Rides Again*) was Linda Stirling. While Frances Gifford and Kay Aldridge drew an occasional raise of the Barbour eyebrow, I was still too young to fully accept them as anything more than general nuisances in their starring serials (*Jungle Girl* for Gifford and *Perils of Nyoka*, *Daredevils of the West*, and *Haunted Harbor* for Aldridge); but I was a little more mature when it came to Linda. She was, in point of fact, the first serial heroine I really enjoyed watching on the screen. Even in her earliest efforts she did a most credible, professional job. Unfortunately, the scriptwriters didn't give her too much of a chance to really demonstrate her versatility (how proficient can you be when you keep getting knocked unconscious chapter after chapter?).

One hates to live in the past, but I must frankly confess that on rare occasions I do sometimes wish I were seated back at the Broadway Theater on a Saturday afternoon with those two bags of *freshly* made popcorn (remember *fresh* popcorn, folks?) watching Kane Richmond, Ralph Byrd, Clayton Moore, Allan Lane, and all the others "do their thing."

Eduardo Ciannelli was the evil Dr. Satan who trapped the Copperhead (Robert Wilcox) in a room whose walls came together in *Mysterious Dr. Satan* (Republic 1940).

Kay Aldridge found herself in this perilous trap in *Perils of Nyoka*
(Republic 1942).

Above: John Hamilton, Kenne Duncan, and Dale Van Sickel
watch as LeRoy Mason is about to unmask Robert Kent and reveal
him as *The Phantom Rider* (Republic 1946). *Below:* "Slingin'
Sammy" Baugh and Duncan Renaldo exposed the villainy of
Neil Hamilton in *King of the Texas Rangers* (Republic 1941).

Opposite page, top: The mysterious villain of the title captures some heavy water to aid in building his deadly Cyclotrode in *The Crimson Ghost* (Republic 1946). *Opposite page, bottom:* Ace stunt man Tom Steele (as the Marvel) traps fellow stunt man Eddie Parker in *The Masked Marvel* (Republic 1943). *Above:* Marten Lamont (in disguise) found himself in George J. Lewis's intricate trap in *Federal Operator 99* (Republic 1945). *Below:* Allan Lane was *King of the Mounties* (Republic 1942) and helped destroy a nest of enemy agents who were using, among other things, this Bat Plane.

Above: Ralph Byrd as Dick Tracy found himself in a blazing inferno in this chapter ending from *Dick Tracy vs. Crime, Inc.* (Republic 1941). *Right:* Marguerite Chapman and Kane Richmond were the stars of *Spy Smasher* (Republic 1942).

Above: In this cliff-hanger Kane Richmond, rather than the obvious dummy, was supposed to be on that ladder pushed off by Bud Geary in *Haunted Harbor* (Republic 1944). *Right:* Linda Stirling, my favorite serial heroine, and George J. Lewis, playing a hero as a change of pace from his usual villainous roles, in *Zorro's Black Whip* (Republic 1944).

Top: Roy Barcroft instructs stunt man Fred Graham and Bud Geary to destroy an explosive device in *The Purple Monster Strikes* (Republic 1945). *Center:* Hero Rod Cameron was subjected to this deadly device in a chapter ending from *Secret Service in Darkest Africa* (Republic 1943). *Bottom:* One of the perils Frances Gifford and Tom Neal faced in *Jungle Girl* (Republic 1941) was the poison gas filling this room.

Right: George Turner as Zorro saves Peggy Stewart from drowning in a chapter resolution from *Son of Zorro* (Republic 1947). *Below:* Bud Wolfe loads the spear gun while Roy Barcroft describes what will happen to Adrian Booth in *Daughter of Don Q* (Republic 1946) if she doesn't cooperate.

Left: In *Manhunt of Mystery Island*
(Republic 1945) Roy Barcroft traps
Richard Bailey and Linda Stirling in a
sealed-off tunnel and instructs his hench-
man to open a valve controlling an
underground river and "drown the rats!"
Below: George J. Lewis, *left,* and stunt man
Tom Steele are trapped by Dick Purcell
as the masked hero in *Captain America*
(Republic 1944).

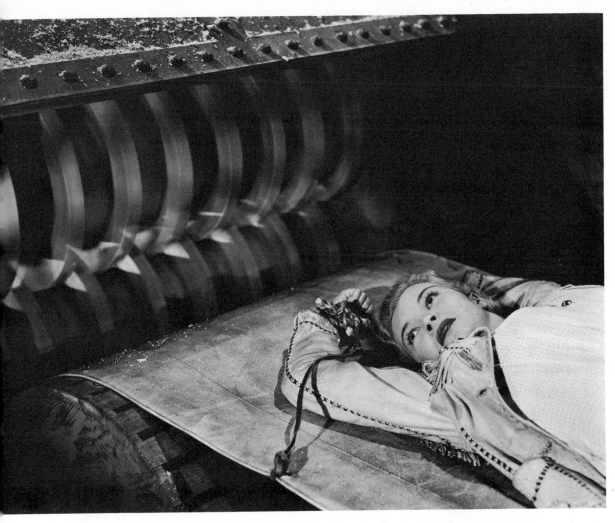

Above: Helen Talbot doesn't appear to enjoy the thought of going into that pulp-shredder in *King of the Forest Rangers* (Republic 1946). *Below:* While Rod Cameron, on the floor, battles Noel Cravat, a deadly spear is set to go off aimed directly at the trapped Constance Worth in this chapter ending from *G-Men vs. The Black Dragon* (Republic 1943).

Above: Carey Loftin, *left,* and Roy Barcroft had Linda
Stirling trapped until Clayton Moore came to the rescue in
Jesse James Rides Again (Republic 1947). *Left:* While
Dale Van Sickel, *left,* battles hero Bruce Edwards in
The Black Widow (Republic 1947), that trunk
(with heroine Virginia Lindley in it) is slated for a long
drop. *Bottom:* Jack Rockwell and Kay Aldridge have just
pulled Allan Lane from a burning death trap in this
chapter resolution from *Daredevils of the West*
(Republic 1943).

Right: Linda Stirling, Republic's most famous serial queen of the forties, in *The Tiger Woman* (Republic 1944).

Allan Lane saves Duncan Renaldo and Linda Stirling just in time from flaming death in a chapter resolution from *The Tiger Woman* (Republic 1944).

Mike Mazurki was the killer who menaced Anne Jeffreys and
Morgan Conway (as Tracy) in the first of four features based on
Chester Gould's famous strip, *Dick Tracy* (RKO 1945).

8.

Murder for the Masses

Almost everyone loves a good mystery film, and though the major studios produced very few quality big-budget whodunnits in the forties, the minor companies were turning them out quite regularly by the dozens, both in series and as individual thrillers. Many of these sixty-minute programmers were not really mysteries in the true sense of the word, but rather straight action dramas which found the films' heroes tracking down various lawbreakers.

My favorite mystery series was the twelve Sherlock Holmes adventures produced by Universal Pictures between 1942 and 1946, starring Basil Rathbone as Holmes and Nigel Bruce as Dr. Watson. Twentieth Century-Fox had produced two excellent Holmes films, *The Hound of the Baskervilles* and *The Adventures of Sherlock Holmes*, also with Rathbone and Bruce, in 1939, setting both of them in period. The Universal series was moved up in time to the forties, and several of the films found Holmes matching wits with wartime enemy agents. *Spider Woman* was very likely the one film in the series that seemed to play theaters on constant reissue. Gale Sondergaard was the woman of the film's title who very nearly put an end to the detective's career by placing him inside a revolving target at a shooting gallery where he was almost shot to death by poor Dr. Watson. Professor Moriarty nearly finished Holmes in *Sherlock Holmes and the Secret Weapon* by attaching a tube to the detective's arm and draining his blood—and life—away drop by drop. Lionel Atwill was an excellent Moriarty, as was Henry Daniell in the later *The Woman in Green*. The adventure in

the series which really pleased me the most was *Sherlock Holmes Faces Death*, loosely based on "The Musgrave Ritual," one of the original stories by Sir Arthur Conan Doyle. Here Holmes helped solve a mystery by moving real people on a giant chessboard painted on one of the floors of a murder-ridden mansion.

One of the most popular radio shows of the forties was *I Love a Mystery*, which told the continued tales of three devil-may-care adventurers, Jack, Doc, and Reggie. When Columbia brought the characters to the screen they dropped Reggie but featured Jim Bannon as Jack and Barton Yarborough (who had played the same character on radio) as Doc. The series was short (only three titles), but enough chills were delivered in *The Devil's Mask*, with our leads following a trail of shrunken heads, to make up for the deficiency in longevity.

Chester Morris was one of the screen's really fine character actors in the thirties, but his fine performances in films like *The Big House*, *Five Came Back*, and *Blind Alley* are usually forgotten by most people who remember him only as that dashing detective with a sense of humor, Boston Blackie. In thirteen films he matched wits, insults and intrigue with Richard Lane as Inspector Faraday. Morris was a fine magician in real life, and he often worked routines into the series, which ran from 1941 through 1949 and included such titles as *Boston Blackie Booked on Suspicion*, *Boston Blackie Goes to Hollywood*, *Confessions of Boston Blackie*, and *The Phantom Thief*.

Another popular radio show of the time was

The Whistler, which featured a mysterious story-teller who weekly announced, "I know many strange stories, for I walk by night." On the screen the Whistler told some really superb tales that featured Richard Dix in the leading roles. Dix was another excellent actor who had appeared mostly in outdoor action films during the thirties and now found himself relegated to B-film duty. In the first film of the series, *The Whistler*, Dix schemed to have a professional killer murder him and then changed his mind, almost too late. Other titles included *The Power of the Whistler*, *The Mark of the Whistler*, *Voice of the Whistler*, and *The Thirteenth Hour*.

Columbia's Crime Doctor series featured Warner Baxter, another fine actor of the thirties now doing routine programmers, as a leading criminal psychologist. In *Crime Doctor*, the first film in the sequence of ten, it was revealed that Dr. Ordway had originally been a criminal himself, but now, as a result of amnesia, was a successful mental practitioner. *The Millerson Case*, *Shadows in the Night*, *The Crime Doctor's Gamble*, and *Crime Doctor's Manhunt* were among the Crime Doctor's more celebrated cases.

The two remaining series turned out by Columbia were also crowd-pleasers. Ralph Bellamy and William Gargan took turns in portraying Ellery Queen in such favorites as *Ellery Queen's Penthouse Mystery* and *A Close Call for Ellery Queen*. Margaret Lindsay was Nikki Porter and Charlie Grapewin played Inspector Queen, with both Bellamy and Gargan in a series that provided considerably more laughs than thrills. Just as Columbia had filled its serials and Westerns with time-consuming, unfunny comic routines, so too did they stress the non-mystery elements in what could have been highly thrilling features. Most of the Lone Wolf films were made in the late thirties, but the studio frequently brought them back to rerun houses in the forties. Warren William was the best of the several actors who portrayed the Michael Lanyard role (others were Melvyn Douglas and Francis Lederer before him, and later Gerald Mohr). Titles included *The Lone Wolf Keeps a Date*, *The Lone Wolf Spy Hunt*, *The Lone Wolf Meets a Lady*, and *The Lone Wolf in Mexico*, among others.

RKO was no slouch when it came to series films, either. It had the Saint with Louis Hayward or George Sanders playing the role in most of the films like *The Saint in New York*, *The Saint in London*, *The Saint in Palm Springs*, while Sanders and his real-life brother Tom Conway gave screen life to the Falcon in a popular string of adventures that included *The Falcon's Brother* (in which both Sanders and Conway appeared), *The Falcon Takes Over*, *The Falcon Strikes Back*, and *The Falcon Out West*. Also from RKO came the four Dick Tracy features (there were also four Republic serials based on the character). The first two, *Dick Tracy* and *Dick Tracy vs. Cueball*, featured Morgan Conway as the comic-strip detective, while Ralph Byrd took over in *Dick Tracy's Dilemma* and *Dick Tracy Meets Gruesome*. Recent screenings have shown the films to be generally routine and dull; most people seem to enjoy *Dilemma* best, because of Jack Lambert's portrayal of the villain with a hook for a hand.

Twentieth Century-Fox was still striking pay-dirt in the forties by reissuing its Charlie Chan and Mr. Moto films made in the thirties. Both series had great production values (usually utilizing the big sets that were built for major Fox films), and Warner Oland and Sidney Toler as Chan and Peter Lorre as Moto always delivered topnotch characterizations. A new series produced by the studio were the Michael Shayne entries featuring Lloyd Nolan as the wisecracking detective in such titles as *The Man Who Wouldn't Die* and *Michael Shayne, Private Detective*. (PRC also had some Shayne adventures a few years later with Hugh Beaumont starring, as well as a short Philo Vance series with Alan Curtis.)

MGM would occasionally come up with another in its popular Thin Man films with William Powell and Myrna Loy again playing Nick and Nora Charles, two sophisticated, debonair, and double-entendre-dropping sleuths in titles like *Song of the Thin Man* and *Shadow of the Thin Man*. All the Thin Man films had excellent production values, although the quality of the mystery content varied.

Paramount contributed its Bulldog Drummond films with John Howard and John Barrymore, and Monogram was turning out its newer Charlie Chans as well as the Shadow and Mr. Wong films (discussed in another chapter).

There were also a great many comedy-mysteries starring such favorites as Milton Berle (*Whispering Ghosts*), Red Skelton (*Whistling in the Dark*, *Whistling in Brooklyn*, and *Whistling in Dixie*, in which he played a radio detective called the Fox), Olsen and Johnson (*Ghost Catchers*), Abbott and Costello (*Who Done It?*), Fred Allen (*It's in the Bag*), and others.

These generally entertaining short films never

pretended to be material of lasting value and quality. They were made quickly to please an audience who wanted the additional advantage of not only watching a film, but participating in it. It was a challenge to match one's knowledge and abilities against those of the heroes on the screen. What matter if the clues were skimpy, the logic often faulty, and the action sometimes routine, as long as we could watch all those great character actors slinking around to try and throw us off the trail? And if we guessed correctly? Well, the smiles and the "I-knew-who-it-was-all-the-time" lines would flow until we had convinced all our boyhood friends that we were really smarter than Philo Vance, Boston Blackie, the Falcon, the Saint, the Lone Wolf, Bulldog Drummond, Charlie Chan, Mr. Moto, Ellery Queen, and all the others combined. And who could deny, with any degree of authority, that we weren't?

Warren William was the urbane detective-hero in *The Lone Wolf Strikes* (Columbia 1940) who apparently had Montagu Love at a disadvantage in this scene from the film.

Top: Ralph Bellamy was one of several actors who played Ellery Queen for laughs and thrills on the screen. This scene is from *Ellery Queen and the Murder Ring* (Columbia 1941). *Center:* Gerald Mohr was the famous detective in *The Lone Wolf in Mexico* (Columbia 1947), aided by the nonsense of Eric Blore. *Bottom:* In *The Whistler* (Columbia 1944), star Richard Dix involves himself in a situation in which he is almost killed.

Left: George Sanders shows an important clue to Jonathan Hale in *The Saint in Palm Springs* (RKO 1941), one in a long line of Saint films with different stars playing the detective. *Below*: Alan Curtis was one of the screen's portrayers of Philo Vance, here seen with Sheila Ryan in *Philo Vance's Secret Mission* (PRC 1947).

Above: Richard Lane, *left,* and Walter Sande think they have Chester Morris
(as Blackie) trapped again, while Lloyd Corrigan, *right,* watches in *After Midnight with
Boston Blackie* (Columbia 1943). *Below, left:* Barry Nelson, *left,* William Powell,
Sam Levene, and Henry O'Neil help solve an important case in *Shadow of the
Thin Man* (MGM 1941). *Below, right:* William Gargan as Ellery is obviously
being amazed again by Margaret Lindsay (as Nikki Porter) in *A Close Call for Ellery
Queen* (Columbia 1942), another in the popular series.

Right: Ralph Byrd played his Dick Tracy role in four serials, two features, and a television series. This scene is from *Dick Tracy's Dilemma* (RKO 1947). *Below:* Dick Tracy's adversary in *Dick Tracy's Dilemma* (RKO 1947) was Jack Lambert, who met his death when his hook touched high-voltage wires.

Above: Lloyd Nolan, *center*, explains an important discovery to Henry Wilcoxon while Marjorie Weaver watches in the Michael Shayne mystery *The Man Who Wouldn't Die* (Twentieth Century-Fox 1942).

Below: Tom Conway as the Falcon, *right*, spies Robert Armstrong up to no good in this scene from *The Falcon in San Francisco* (RKO 1945).

Top: Basil Rathbone and Nigel Bruce discover a murdered Halliwell Hobbes in *Sherlock Holmes Faces Death* (Universal 1943). *Bottom:* Alec Craig ushers Basil Rathbone into a waiting trap set by the *Spider Woman* (Universal 1944), played by Gale Sondergaard.

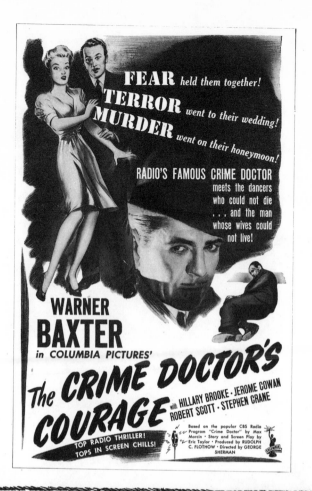

FEAR *held them together!*
TERROR *went to their wedding!*
MURDER *went on their honeymoon!*

RADIO'S FAMOUS CRIME DOCTOR meets the dancers who could not die ...and the man whose wives could not live!

WARNER BAXTER
in COLUMBIA PICTURES'

The CRIME DOCTOR'S COURAGE

with HILLARY BROOKE · JEROME COWAN
ROBERT SCOTT · STEPHEN CRANE

Based on the popular CBS Radio Program "Crime Doctor" by Max Marcin · Story and Screen Play by Eric Taylor · Produced by RUDOLPH C. FLOTHOW · Directed by GEORGE SHERMAN

TOP RADIO THRILLER!
TOPS IN SCREEN CHILLS!

"THERE'S BLOOD ON THE MOON TONIGHT!"

THRILLS!
HORROR!
...as the mystery wizards tackle a trackless terror!

BASIL RATHBONE
as Sherlock Holmes
NIGEL BRUCE
as Dr. Watson
in

THE SCARLET CLAW

with KAY HARDING
GERALD HAMER
PAUL CAVANAGH
ARTHUR HOHL
MILES MANDER

Realart
RE-RELEASE

Above: Basil Rathbone, *right*, catches a disguised killer (Gerald Hamer) in the Sherlock Holmes adventure *The Scarlet Claw* (Universal 1944). *Below:* I wonder if the Crime Doctor (Warner Baxter, *left*) can talk his way out of being shot by Steven Geray in *The Crime Doctor's Gamble* (Columbia 1947).

Reginald Denny, *left*, John Howard (as Drummond), E. E. Clive, and John
Barrymore were the stars of *Bulldog Drummond's Revenge* (Paramount 1937).

Tom Conway, *left*, and George Sanders were real-life brothers who appeared together in *The Falcon's Brother* (RKO 1942) with Jane Randolph.

John Carradine shows Mr. Moto (Peter Lorre, *left*) an important clue in
Thank You, Mr. Moto (Twentieth Century-Fox 1937).

Above: Wally Vernon looks astonished while Sidney Toler, *right*, looks only interested in a trick by Cesar Romero in *Charlie Chan on Treasure Island* (Twentieth Century-Fox 1939), from which this publicity photo is taken. *Below:* Jim Bannon, *center,* was Jack and Barton Yarborough, *right,* was Doc in the *I Love a Mystery* adventure *The Devil's Mask* (Columbia 1946). That's Paul Burns polishing up a fang or two.

Above: Red Skelton shows co-star Ann Rutherford a mysterious clue in *Whistling in Dixie* (MGM 1942).
Opposite page, top: Ole Olsen and Chic Johnson were a couple of zany *Ghost Catchers* (Universal 1944).
Opposite page, bottom: Brenda Joyce and Milton Berle bump into mysterious John Carradine in this scene from *Whispering Ghosts* (Twentieth Century-Fox 1942).

William Elliott was Red Ryder and Bobby Blake Little Beaver in a popular series of action adventures turned out by Republic Pictures in the forties.

9.
Dusty Trails to Adventure

To me, one of the most exciting and beautiful sights on the motion picture screen is that of a horse running full tilt photographed against the background of the scenic splendor of the American Southwest. Even in my early days of moviegoing this element of the B-Western films seems to have overshadowed all the usual action embellishments of the genre. Though, as in the case of the serials, I preferred the product turned out by Republic, considering it of higher entertainment value action-wise, I allowed myself to be greedily self-indulgent to the point of enjoying almost all Westerns no matter which studio turned them out.

My first Western idol on the screen was Don "Red" Barry (he had gained the nickname after appearing in the serial *Adventures of Red Ryder*), a short, tough, and thoroughly professional actor who looked excellent in the saddle and performed his dialogue scenes with credible justice. The Barry Westerns were mostly tautly wrought little gems that often stressed the dramatic rather than physical conflicts in the stories. In several of his films Barry played a dual role (usually twin brothers, one bad through circumstances beyond his control, and one good who was invariably a preacher, lawyer, or doctor). He claims to have encouraged Republic to give him these double-duty efforts in order to showcase his acting capabilities. After all, as we all know, the meaty roles in these minor Westerns almost always were plum assignments meted out to the likes of Roy Barcroft, Charles King, Harry

Woods, LeRoy Mason, and similar specialists in the gentle art of chicanery.

Following close on Barry's heels was William "Wild Bill" Elliott (like Barry, he had picked up his middle tag from a character he played in a serial and series of Westerns, Wild Bill Hickok). Elliott had begun his screen career by playing fancy-dressed dudes in scores of minor bit roles in the thirties before finally getting his chance to star in Westerns and serials at Columbia. When he finally moved over to Republic in the early forties, the studio starred him in a series of eight actioners paired with George "Gabby" Hayes (my favorite cowboy sidekick). After that brief series, he was chosen to star in sixteen features based on the exploits of Fred Harmon's famous comic-strip cowboy, Red Ryder, and it is this group of films he is best remembered for. Many of the sixteen films are among the best that the studio ever turned out, each full of thrilling chases, fights, and assorted action all backed by excellent musical scores, mostly composed by Mort Glickman. Remember Red's sidekick, Little Beaver? The role was played by Bobby Blake who, under the name Robert Blake, achieved an outstanding personal success in the film *In Cold Blood* in the middle sixties (his publicity proclaimed him as a *"new"* screen sensation, even though he had appeared in films regularly since the early forties, including such classics as *The Treasure of the Sierra Madre*, in which he sold Bogart the winning lottery ticket that set the film's plot in motion). After the

Ryder series Elliott was bumped upstairs to star in big-budget pictures in which he was never really used effectively. Most of us wished he had remained as Red Ryder, uttering his famous tag line, "I'm a peaceable man, but—"

Picking up the Ryder reins for seven more films was Allan Lane, who had finished his serial duties and his own series of six relatively adventurous efforts. When Republic finally threw in the towel as far as the Ryder character was concerned (after twenty-three features and one serial) Lane tacked on a new nickname and as Allan "Rocky" Lane went on to be a leading Western star until the studio ceased production in 1955.

In the middle forties Sunset Carson made a very impressive entry into the action film sweepstakes, and there are those who claim that he was actually outpulling Roy Rogers in the fan-mail received by the studio from the southern states. I can believe it. Carson was a huge six-foot-four-plus, no-nonsense cowboy whose mainstay was action. No guitar-playing, fancy-dressed drugstore cowboy, he was a rugged ready-made audience-pleaser. Unfortunately, because of personal problems his tenure at Republic was all too brief.

Monogram was turning out some pretty respectable thrillers itself. Johnny Mack Brown was featured in a memorable series which, in almost every case, found him riding into a town (usually using the name Nevada) and bumping into his pal Raymond Hatton (called Sandy Hopkins). Unfortunately, not much money was budgeted for the productions, and the interior sets were usually skimpy and cheap-looking; but once outside, Johnny, expert horseman that he was, made the films a sheer joy to watch. I don't think any cowboy actor was ever able to throw such a realistic-looking punch in a fight sequence as Johnny. Even Yakima Canutt, the king of stunt men, admits that his favorite people to work with were John Wayne and Johnny Mack Brown.

Hatton retained his Sandy Hopkins label when he joined pals Buck Jones and Tim McCoy in the very popular Rough Riders series. The two things I remember most about those films were Buck's chewing a stick of gum whenever he was getting ready for some fast action, and the scene that closed each film where the three comrades rode off in different directions after having completed their latest mission.

Trios seemed to be very popular in those early-forties days. Republic continued its popular Three Mesquiteers series which had been so successful in the thirties (unfortunately, the original trio of Ray Corrigan, Bob Livingston, and Max Terhune had departed and their replacements, Bob Steele, Tom Tyler, and Rufe Davis didn't seem to possess the same magic), and Monogram brought back Hoot Gibson, Bob Steele, and Ken Maynard as the Trail Blazers. Although Steele was still adept at his work, Ken and Hoot were well past their prime, and it was almost grotesque at times to see them try to recapture the glory they had once possessed as individual stars. The Range Busters were another popular trio who managed to provide occasional thrills. Comprised of Ray Corrigan, Max Terhune, and John King, the Range Busters often seemed to spend a great deal more time clowning around than fighting. One of the films in the series, *Saddle Mountain Roundup*, was really a very exciting little mystery-Western, complete with secret caves and a mysterious murderer. It even was published in one of the popular Big Little Books (remember those, folks?).

And there were numerous other stars who rode the range for our entertainment. Some of them, like Buster Crabbe with his sidekick Al "Fuzzy" St. John, William Boyd as Hopalong Cassidy, and Charles Starrett as the Durango Kid, were excellent, while others such as Jimmy Wakely, Eddie Dean, Whip Wilson, Lash La-Rue, and Monte Hale just couldn't quite cut it.

But of all the Western stars of the forties, the two most popular in general appeal were Roy Rogers and Gene Autry. In the thirties Autry was probably *the* biggest B-Western star, and his recordings sold in the millions. While Autry was stashing away a fortune, Rogers was still a member of the Sons of the Pioneers singing group, and he made appearances in several of Autry's early films in singing or bit roles. In the late thirties Rogers had started his own series and was moving up fast on Autry, who was still riding high into the early forties. When war broke out Gene enlisted in the Air Force, and Republic quickly moved Roy in to fill the gap. Within a year Rogers was in fact as well as in title the "King of the Cowboys." Both Autry's and Rogers' features were usually given deluxe theater treatment in Oakland on their initial releases. They seldom appeared at the regular run-of-the-mill "scratch-houses" that fans like myself frequented, but rather as the companion features at the big first-run houses; thus I missed a great

Above: Eddie Dean delivers a right cross to Eddie Parker in *Shadow Valley*
(PRC 1947). Lying across the desk is veteran Western badman George Chesebro.
Below: The Range Busters, Max "Alibi" Terhune, *left*, Ray "Crash" Corrigan, and
John "Dusty" King listen to Riley Hill disclose some important information in
Texas Trouble Shooters (Monogram 1942).

Above: Smiley Burnette and Noah Beery, Sr., watched and listened as
Gene Autry strummed and sang the title song in *Mexicali Rose* (Republic
1939). *Below:* Roy Rogers, *left*, and Gene Autry, *right*, flank Allen Wilson,
a vice-president in charge of production for Republic Pictures, in a rare
photo of the two stars together. Immediately behind Roy is one of the
top action directors, William Witney.

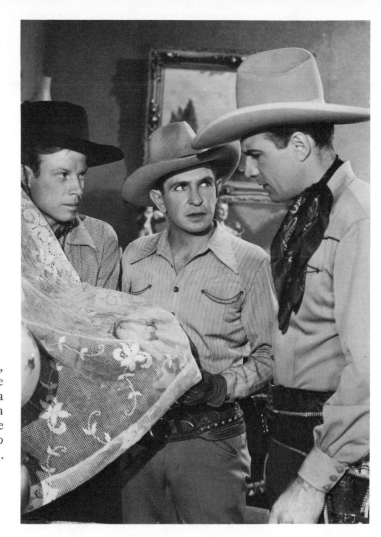

Right: In *Thundering Trails* (Republic 1943), Jimmy Dodd, *left*, Bob Steele, and Tom Tyler were the popular Three Mesquiteers who solved a murder mystery. *Below:* Roy Rogers, *left*, had a terrific battle with stunt man David Sharpe at the conclusion of *Bells of San Angelo* (Republic 1947).

many of them (which I fortunately saw many years later when they were all sold to television). The films of both men vary in quality a great deal. Usually the studio would produce a series of eight films per year featuring each star. Four to six of the films would be done on skimpy budgets and would be filmed primarily on the studio's back lot, and the remainder would get the deluxe treatment which included additional songs (with some production value), more picturesque exterior locations, more bit-players, better costumes, higher-caliber villains and about fifteen minutes added running time (most of their films hovered around the sixty-five minute mark, but some of these specials ran as long as eighty-seven minutes). One of the best of the Rogers' "spectaculars" was *Silver Spurs*, made in 1943, which featured John Carradine as the principal heavy. The film was beautifully photographed against the background of the Sierra Nevada Mountains and featured a thrilling wagon chase replete with ace stunt work as an entertaining finale. As the forties moved along, Rogers' films began to lose their tendency to be primarily aimed at juvenile audiences. When men like Sloan Nibley moved in to take over the scripting chores, the films became more rugged, the violence more pronounced (for example, Roy Barcroft's mercilessly dumping oil cans filled with smuggled aliens into a lake in *The Far Frontier*, or Dale Van Sickel and David Sharpe as they gave Roy one helluva working over in *Bells of San Angelo*) and the dialogue more realistic. Other newly acquired assets were the use of Trucolor and the directorial services of William Witney. Witney was, and continues to be, one of the top action directors around (his handling of the Republic serials in the late thirties and early forties gave them their distinctive action-packed style), and he kept Rogers' films moving along at an audience-pleasing, fast-paced clip.

When Autry returned after his war service, Rogers was now top man at Republic, and rivalry was bound to emerge. Gene made only one short series for the studio, which had made him a star, and then moved over to Columbia Pictures, where he was able not only to star in but produce his own films. Both men retained their enormous popularity into the fifties (each made records, had radio shows, and produced their own television half-hour series) and Roy is still a popular attraction (teamed with his wife and frequent co-star in many of his films, Dale Evans) for even today's audiences.

The B-Western is now a relic of those good old days, seldom seen except on television stations that have the courage to run them for those of us who remember (no New York station has run a Republic B-Western in the eleven years I have lived here), and a few scattered theaters in the southern states that still cater to kids who crave a little action. Station-owners claim that the B-Western has been replaced by the hour-long television show like *Gunsmoke* and *Bonanza*. Surely they must be mistaken. Under *no* circumstances were the B-Westerns *ever* as dull and actionless as those television talk-a-thons. May I suggest to those very same "authorities" on public taste that, if they want to turn out some superior action fare, they hire William Witney—FAST!

Above: In *A Missouri Outlaw* (Republic 1941),
Don "Red" Barry tracked down four killers who were
responsible for a sheriff's death. All four, including
John Merton in this scene, wind up destroying themselves.
Right: Tex Ritter was a very popular star in Monogram
films and over at Universal where he made some
popular features with Johnny Mack Brown.

Left: Sunset Carson was a popular success at Republic in the mid-forties. *Below:* Tim Holt, *right,* ties up Cy Kendall and Ernie Adams in this scene from *The Fargo Kid* (RKO 1940).

Above: Allan Lane as Red Ryder helps Roy Barcroft up
after having just given him a beating, while Tom London, *left*,
Gene Roth and Trevor Bardette watch in *Marshal of
Cripple Creek* (Republic 1947). *Below, left:* Charles Starrett
was the Durango Kid in *Challenge of the Range* (Columbia
1949) and dozens of other Western adventures featuring
the same character. *Below, right:* Tom Keene, *left*, listens to
some advice from LeRoy Mason in *Painted Trail* (Monogram
1938), one of a series of fine films Keene made for
RKO and Monogram.

Above: Al "Fuzzy" St. John, *left,* and pal Lash LaRue talk things over in *Cheyenne Takes Over* (PRC 1947). *Below:* Monte Hale mixes it up with stunt ace David Sharpe in *California Firebrand* (Republic 1948).

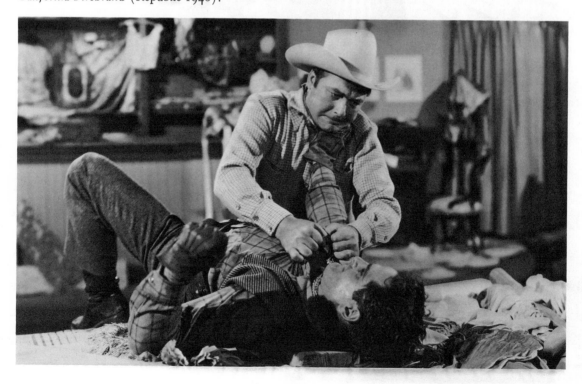

Above: Ghost Town Law (Monogram 1942) featured Buck Jones, *left*, Tim McCoy, and Raymond Hatton as the Rough Riders. *Below:* Rod Cameron, *right*, gets tough with George Eldredge while veteran badman Edmund Cobb watches in *The Old Texas Trail* (Universal 1944).

Opposite page: Raymond Hatton was Sandy Hopkins to Johnny Mack Brown's Nevada or Jack McKenzie in a whole series for Monogram. This scene is from *Land of the Lawless* (Monogram 1947). *Above:* George Houston gets the drop on Glenn Strange in *Lone Rider and the Bandit* (PRC 1942). Houston wanted to be an operatic singer and was making cheap Westerns to get money to form his own company, but he died a premature death before he could achieve his ambition. *Below:* Eddy Waller, *left,* and Allan "Rocky" Lane ask veteran cowboy star Bob Steele some questions in *Savage Frontier* (Republic 1953).

Douglas Fairbanks, Jr., was the daredevil Irish adventurer in *The Fighting O'Flynn* (Universal 1948), one of the films he produced himself.

10.

New Worlds to Conquer

Who among us hasn't at one time or another in our young lives wished that he or she had lived in another period of history? With razor-sharp rapier we could quickly have dispatched the likes of Basil Rathbone, George Macready, and Henry Daniell, or traveled to an exotic South Sea Island paradise in search of giant pearls and adventure. Movie screens in the early forties were full of exciting escapist films which more than satisfied our cravings for new and thrilling worlds to vicariously conquer.

The king of the great movie swashbucklers was, of course, Errol Flynn, and his dashing presence was available to us in constant reissues of his classic adventures like *Captain Blood, The Sea Hawk,* and *Adventures of Robin Hood.* I had some mixed feelings about the first two films, both of which seemed long and talky except for the thrilling dueling scenes, but I had unabashed enthusiasm for all of *Robin Hood.* Filmed in beautiful Technicolor, who could fail to enjoy this classic tale of Robin and his Merry Men with its fabulous castles, archery tournaments, lavish banquets, and one of the most famous fencing matches in screen history? Who could ever forget Errol and Basil Rathbone as they fought each other on winding staircases, over furniture, and through hallways, with their shadows playing grotesque pantomimes on the columns and walls of the mammoth castle set? And, naturally, as they dueled they threw jeering lines at one another (Rathbone: "You've come to Nottingham once too often, my friend"; Flynn: "After today there'll be no need for me to come again!").

Robin Hood must surely be classified among the top ten entertainment-action films of all time.

Much as I admired Flynn, however, my real hero in those years of the forties was Douglas Fairbanks, Jr. Fairbanks, with that incredibly infectious smile and the animated jauntiness he surely inherited from his famous father, never failed to thrill me in his classic adventures. In *The Corsican Brothers* he had the pleasure of competing with himself as he played the dual role of the Siamese twin brothers who, separated at birth, continue to feel and suffer each other's emotions. Both brothers fought against the tyranny of Akim Tamiroff and his evil henchman, John Emery (as well as fighting each other), until, in the end, one brother sacrifices his life for the other. In *The Exile* Fairbanks was an exiled king who was hounded by a satanically portrayed Henry Daniell, whom Doug dispatched in a spectacular battle with swords in an old windmill. *The Fighting O'Flynn* found our dashing hero fighting with flashing grin and pistols against the oppression being perpetrated by Richard Greene in the Ireland of the 1800s. This film had a rousing battle in a castle parapet with exploding fireworks going off all over the place as its finale. But the best film Fairbanks made in the forties, I still feel, was *Sinbad the Sailor.* Here was glorious color adventure on a grand scale. Fairbanks, as the famed storyteller of the *Arabian Nights,* was in top form as he related this tale of a search for fabulous treasure on a mysterious island. Around to oppose him were Anthony Quinn and Walter Slezak, and the film seemed just chock-full of chases, sea battles, duels, and romantic adventure. I remember my father taking me to San Francisco to see the film, and I could never forget the exciting finale, which found Doug being pursued by Quinn in a furious sea chase. Fairbanks loads a catapulting device with a solid ball of flaming tar and fires it at Quinn's boat, and the screen becomes crimson as we see cross-cutting between the ball of flame coming directly at the camera and the brightening red face of the terrified Quinn until the final dazzling fade-out. Much as I love Fairbanks, however, I do wish he would quit saying on television and elsewhere that he did all his own stunt work. All true aficionados know that many of the spectacular leaps and stunts were, in fact, done by David Sharpe (who actually received second-unit credit on screen for *The Exile*), that great stunt man who enlivened so many serials and features through the years.

Tyrone Power wasn't bad in his few swashbuckling efforts, but his *The Mark of Zorro* I found strangely unappealing, even seeing it as a tolerant child. Whereas Douglas Fairbanks's silent version had been simply full of daredevil stunts and chases, this remake had very little of that sort of thing. The stress was put on the dialogue sequences to the detriment of the action episodes, and the film suffered for it. There was, nevertheless, that memorable duel, perhaps one of the best ever done, between Power and Basil Rathbone. Rathbone loved fencing as a personal hobby, and his enthusiasm is quite evident. Power's other major entry in the action field during this period was *The Black Swan*, a real thriller of a pirate picture that has too seldom been presented on screens and television.

Another popular favorite was Louis Hayward. Having a very likable personality, not unlike that of Flynn and Fairbanks, Hayward entertained us in such pleasant divertissements as *The Black Arrow* and *The Return of Monte Cristo*. His real classics, however, were *The Man in the Iron Mask*, in which he played a delightful dual role as twin brothers vying for a throne, one of whom imprisons the other in a grotesque iron mask so that no one will ever discover the resemblance between the two, and *The Son of Monte Cristo*, in which he led a daredevil bunch of patriots in opposing the rule of a smirking George Sanders. I'll never forget the final action scene where Sanders, slain by Hayward in a duel, falls over a balcony and plunges spectacularly through an ornate glass window to a floor many feet below.

The Son of Monte Cristo used to come back to theaters quite regularly paired with the original *The Count of Monte Cristo*, made in 1934. This early film is quite a classic itself. Although it possesses some good action sequences, the most important attributes of the film are the superb performances of its stars, primarily Robert Donat as the Count. Donat, easily one of the finest actors of all time, had a field day as the sailor who is unjustly sent to prison (by the intrigue of Raymond Walburn, Sidney Blackmer, and Louis Calhern), escapes after nearly twenty years' imprisonment and returns to seek vengeance against the plotters. One might have wished that Donat would have lent his charm and talent to more films of this type.

For jungle devotees, there were, of course, numerous Tarzan adventures. MGM, which had turned out the best films in the series in the thirties, kept bringing back their early adventures in reissues, but it is the RKO entries I recall enjoying the most. This was probably because these later films were full of so many relatively silly gimmicks and situations. In *Tarzan's Desert Mystery*, for example, I remember Boy (Johnny Sheffield) being trapped in a giant spider web, while the web's creator came menacingly close to having a delicious repast until Tarzan arrived in the nick of time. Perhaps all kids are a little sadistic at heart (didn't we all applaud when heroes threw villains off cliffs or destroyed them in other similarly spectacular ways?), and my crowd at the theaters always got a bang out of seeing Tarzan—or his opponents—winding up in quicksand or man-eating plants. Ah, the thrill of it all!

Giant pearls were the ultimate goal of Victor McLaglen and his band of merry cutthroats in the very popular *South of Pago Pago*. They traveled to a remote tropic paradise where Jon Hall tried desperately to convince his people that they shouldn't dive into the extreme depths where the big pearls lay. Needless to say, McLaglen cajoled the natives into diving anyway, and one of the poor devils managed to get his foot caught in the gaping jaws of a giant oyster and was saved just in time by Hall who, after some pressure on his own, convinced his friends to do away with McLaglen and his bunch.

And, finally, there was Cornel Wilde. Wilde has turned into one of the fine actors of our day in the adventure field (no one can ever forget *The Naked Prey*), but in those days he was a yet untrained caricature of the great dashing heroes like Flynn, Hayward, and Fairbanks. *The Bandit of Sherwood Forest* found him playing the son of the famed inhabitant of the greenwood and opposing the villainy of George Macready. There were many excellent riding sequences, and the splendid use of color enhanced the entire production. The ending was a memorable one, which found Macready locking Wilde up as a prisoner and then challenging him to a duel, but depriving him of food and water so that he would be too weak to really be able to fight. Unfortunately, Macready hadn't counted on the cleverness of Anita Louise, who managed to smuggle water and food to Wilde from an adjoining cell, and the battle was thus joined on equal terms with our dashing hero winning duel and fair maiden. A *Thousand and One Nights* was both a pleasure and an annoyance to watch. Another excellent color production, for me the film had far too many laughs (admittedly it was made for laughs) and not enough action. Rex Ingram, who had played the Genie in *The Thief of Bagdad* several years before, was back to do similar duty

in this fantasy which found Wilde constantly being annoyed by a female with magical powers (Evelyn Keyes) and a silly Phil Silvers. The pacing was frenetic as Wilde kept losing and regaining his magical powers to the delight of most of the audience.

Larry Parks, who had scored so well in *The Jolson Story*, tried his hand at becoming a new action hero in *The Swordsman* and *The Gallant Blade*, but in fact he was amazingly bland and uninspiring. By the time he had arrived on the screen, the great days of daring rogues had pretty well vanished. The closest the screen ever got to those great action heroes of the early forties came almost a decade later in the person of Stewart Granger. He alone seemed to inspire that great feeling for adventure we all lusted after in such superior works as *The Prisoner of Zenda* (an almost exact scene-for-scene remake of the famous Ronald Colman version of the thirties) and *Scaramouche* (which featured one of the longest, if not *the* longest, dueling sequence in screen history). Flynn, Fairbanks, Hayward, Wilde, Granger—I wonder if we shall ever see their like upon the screen again.

Tyrone Power was the masked avenger in the sound remake of
The Mark of Zorro (Twentieth Century-Fox 1940). The film lacked much
of the excitement of the silent version, and dialogue sequences
became boring after a while to young audiences.

Above: Douglas Fairbanks, Jr., and Joan Bennett in the jungle adventure *Green Hell* (Universal 1940). If that set looks familiar to you, it's because you saw it, slightly altered, in *The Mummy's Hand* (Universal 1940), a scene from which appears in chapter four of this book. *Right*: Errol Flynn and Basil Rathbone fought their first screen duel together in *Captain Blood* (Warner Bros 1935).

Left: Louis Hayward played a dual role in
The Man in the Iron Mask (Small-United Artists
1939). This is a shot of him as Philippe. *Below:*
Warren William, *left,* and Alan Hale fight to free
Louis Hayward from his devilish mask in *The Man
in the Iron Mask* (Small-United Artists 1939).

Opposite page, above: Jon Hall and Frances
Farmer were the young lovers in South of Pago
Pago (Small-United Artists 1940), an adventure
film about men in search of giant pearls. Opposite
page, below: Clayton Moore, left, and Montagu
Love assisted masked Louis Hayward in his fight
to overthrow evil George Sanders in The Son of
Monte Cristo (Small-United Artists 1940).
Above: Basil Rathbone and Errol Flynn in the
famous dueling sequence from Adventures of
Robin Hood (Warner Brothers 1938). Right:
Douglas Fairbanks, Jr., was the fantastic story-
teller who told his most exciting tale in Sinbad
the Sailor (RKO 1947).

Opposite page, far left: Larry Parks, who had done so well playing the famous singer in *The Jolson Story* (Columbia 1946), was less successful as a swashbuckler in films like *The Swordsman* (Columbia 1948) and as shown here, *The Gallant Blade* (Columbia 1948). *Opposite page, above:* Frances Gifford and Johnny Weissmuller in *Tarzan Triumphs* (RKO 1943), one of a long string of adventures of the famous ape man made in the forties. *Opposite page, below:* Errol Flynn with sword in hand again as the star of *The Sea Hawk* (Warner Brothers 1940). *Above:* Rex Ingram recreated his role of the Genie, which he had played in *The Thief of Bagdad* (Korda-United Artists 1940), for *A Thousand and One Nights* (Columbia 1945). That's star Cornel Wilde in reduced circumstances in this publicity still from the film.

Above: If one Douglas Fairbanks, Jr., was a treat, two were even better. Here they are in a publicity photo with Ruth Warrick for *The Corsican Brothers* (Small-United Artists 1941). *Below:* George Macready, scar and all, greets Barbara Britton in *The Return of Monte Cristo* (Columbia 1946) while a heavily disguised Louis Hayward watches.

Robert Donat brought his considerable acting skill to the role of Edmond
Dantes in *The Count of Monte Cristo* (Small-United Artists 1934).

Opposite page, top: Louis Hayward again matched wits and swords with George Macready, center, in *The Black Arrow* (Columbia 1948). That's veteran character actor Walter Kingsford looking on. *Opposite page, bottom:* Douglas Fairbanks, Jr., has just finished a duel to the death with Henry Daniell in an old windmill in *The Exile* (Universal 1947). Produced by Fairbanks, the film was one of the few to be made in the forties in Sepia color. *Above:* In *The Bandit of Sherwood Forest* (Columbia 1946), Russell Hicks was the elder Robin Hood and Cornel Wilde his daring son.

Thrill TO THE SPECTACULAR DARING OF THE KING OF Romance AND Adventure!

...he lived as he loved...

dangerously!

Universal-International In Association With The Fairbanks Company Inc. Presents

MARIA MONTEZ

and Introduces

PAULE CROSET

with HENRY DANIELL

NIGEL BRUCE   ROBERT COOTE

and DOUGLAS FAIRBANKS, Jr.

in THE EXILE

Written and Produced by DOUGLAS FAIRBANKS, Jr.
Directed by MAX OPULS • A UNIVERSAL-INTERNATIONAL RELEASE

Veteran actor Harry Carey and
John Wayne in the excellent
The Shepherd of the Hills
(Paramount 1941).

II.
Man of Action

Few people would disagree that John Wayne is probably the single greatest action star in sound-film history. In his forty years of film-making he has made over one hundred and fifty features, almost all of which were full of thrills and excitement. He has had a fluctuating career that has seen frequent moments of screen glory and dismal moments of quickly forgotten failures. For every *Red River* and *True Grit* there has been a *Tycoon* and *Without Reservations*. A success in *The Big Trail* in 1930, he went on to do quickie B's at Mascot, Warner Bros, Monogram, and Republic. *Stagecoach* brought him back to prominence in 1939 and he never slipped back into the co-feature category again. It is not the Wayne of *She Wore a Yellow Ribbon* and *Rio Grande* that I remember from those affectionate matinee days, however—my visions are of the gun-toting war hero winning World War II in *Back to Bataan, Flying Tigers,* and *The Fighting Seabees,* and the skilled horseman who took great delight in brawling to the finish with such worthy opponents as Ward Bond, Randolph Scott, and Albert Dekker.

Most of those action years of the early forties were spent at Republic, but from time to time Duke would venture off that home range to turn in some smashing portrayals at other studios. At Universal he starred in *Seven Sinners, The Spoilers,* and *Pittsburgh.* The first film found him falling temporarily in love with Marlene Dietrich and having a spectacular fight with Oscar Homolka; the second found him falling in permanent love with Marlene Dietrich and having a classic

brawl with Randolph Scott; and the third found him falling out of love with Marlene Dietrich and battling Scott one more time. All three films were very well produced, and by any standards are among the most entertaining action films ever produced.

At RKO Wayne gave credible performances in *A Lady Takes a Chance* with Jean Arthur, in which he played a rodeo cowboy she fell for; *Tall in the Saddle,* in which Ella Raines finally corraled him, but only after many shenanigans and a brutal battle with Ward Bond; and *Back to Bataan,* where, with the help of Anthony Quinn, he helped win a victory in the Philippines.

In *Reap the Wild Wind,* done at Paramount, he was excellent as the skipper who wrecked his own ship on a reef in order to help Raymond Massey and his bunch of salvagers collect a supposed fortune. Filmed in beautiful Technicolor, the film had many spectacular moments, including the famous underwater sequence in which Ray Milland and Wayne battle a giant squid and the latter gives up his life to save his screen rival.

For sheer adventure and excitement, however, it was the work Wayne did at Republic that I really thrived on. In roughly five years Wayne turned out more than a dozen fine action films. Even the ones which were weak in story line, like *Wheel of Fortune, Lady from Louisiana, Lady for a Night,* and *Flame of the Barbary Coast* had many thrilling chase and fight sequences, while the big epics like *Flying Tigers, The Fighting Seabees,* and *In Old Oklahoma* (retitled *War of the Wildcats* in television prints) contained more excitement than the audience really deserved at one time.

Over the years I had often wondered what it was about *Flying Tigers* and *The Fighting Seabees* that made them stand out so prominently as war films. The answer lay not in the excellent performances of Wayne and his supporting cast, but in the superb special effects created by the late Howard Lydecker. I can't recall any war film that had quite so many spectacular effects as these two films. The pyrotechnics were simply dazzling. In *Flying Tigers* Wayne was in command of the famed unit which was fighting the enemy in China before we officially entered World War II. Into the group comes dashing John Carroll, who manages through his own carelessness to make a general mess out of everything, including causing the death of Wayne's closest friend, Paul Kelly. To redeem himself, Carroll takes off on a suicide mission with Wayne to bomb an important bridge. During the attack Carroll is mortally wounded, but he manages to let Wayne get out of the plane in a parachute while he plunges the plane into an enemy train. I can still remember all the close-ups in that film of the grinning Japanese pilots being shot down with blood running from their mouths. We seemed to take sadistic pleasure in watching the enemy bleed a lot. The aerial sequences were the real highlights of this film. Unlike many of the studios who shot their miniatures indoors against painted backdrops, Republic used large-size scale models, meticulously detailed, and photographed them outdoors against actual backgrounds. The difference was like night and day. Next time you see a Universal war film, pay particular attention to the tiny bathtub-like models and you will see the very considerable difference.

In *The Fighting Seabees* it was Wayne's turn to be the pain in the neck who winds up sacrificing his life in a spectacular way. As Wedge Donovan, Wayne was the tough head of a construction company who joins with Dennis O'Keefe, playing a naval officer, to form the Seabees, an advance contingent of engineers and construction men who go in to build airfields and other necessary structures to assist the invasion forces. Because they are untrained and undisciplined, O'Keefe refuses to let them arm themselves, and they are nearly annihilated obeying Wayne's orders. Wedge finally gives in and allows his men to be trained, but the continually aggressive enemy snipers keep popping off his men one by one until he can stand it no longer. The final

blow comes when William Frawley is calmly singing a song as he turns the valve on a just-completed pipeline (you *knew* the minute he started to sing he was bound to get nailed), and an enemy soldier kills him. Wedge again leads his men on a charge and when he leaves camp the enemy decides to attack. The battle is on, and Wayne finally heads back to camp with his men to fight. He decides on a daring plan: to strap a stick of dynamite on the front of a bulldozer and ram it into a tank of oil which will flood the valley with flame and destroy the enemy. He boards the bulldozer (the name "Natasha" was written on it, for those trivia buffs who care!) and aims it at the tank, but an enemy bullet cuts him down and he dies as the inevitable crash and explosion occurs. Lydecker actually filled acres of California real estate with blazing fuel oil to create this spectacular finale. All in all, these are two rousing war films that I find unforgettable.

In *Dark Command* Wayne was a Texas cowboy who came to Kansas and found himself opposing Walter Pidgeon in an important election. Pidgeon, as Will Cantrell, forms a group of terrorists who pillage the area, and is himself finally destroyed in a spectacularly staged gun battle in which almost an entire town goes up in flame. Adding to the excitement was a good performance by Roy Rogers, in one of his few appearances outside of his own starring films, and a thrilling wagon chase ending in a famous stunt sequence in which four stunt men leap from the wagon just as it plunges over a cliff into a lake far below.

In Old Oklahoma had one of the best mass-action chases the screen had seen in a long time. In order to fulfill an oil contract (after many battles, both verbal and physical, with Albert Dekker), Wayne has to deliver a large quantity of the black gold to a distant city. Dekker buys up the only pipeline and forces Wayne to load the volatile fluid in dozens of wagons. The wagons rush across the open plains in a gigantic race against time, with Dekker's henchmen destroying a great many as the deadline approaches. It was a stunt man's delight, with overturning wagons vacated by leaping men showing up all over the place. To add more peril, a giant prairie fire is started and some of the wagons catch aflame (with one plunging spectacularly over a cliff and exploding in mid-air just moments after Wayne's stunt double had unhitched the horses) and are destroyed. But, to no one's real surprise, and with the help of Martha Scott, who keeps Dekker busy, Wayne meets the deadline. Helping the picture to no small extent was a really first-rate musical score by Mort Glickman.

Dakota had action, but it also had Vera Ralston, and I am not sure if even the thrills could overshadow her simply awful performance. *In Old California*, *Lady for a Night*, and *Three Faces West* were interesting but relatively routine, while *Flame of the Barbary Coast* had the considerable benefit of good performances by Ann Dvorak and Joseph Schildkraut and a good (but not as good as Republic should have produced) earthquake sequence.

After five solid years of slam-bang action at Republic, Wayne finally was given an excellent chance to show his versatility in *Angel and the Badman* in 1947. As Quirt Evans, Wayne played

the role of a hunted outlaw who was hounded and almost killed until he found help and contentment on the farm of a Quaker family. Gail Russell (who was to star with Wayne in that moody, psychological oddity, *Wake of the Red Witch*, for Republic the following year) was excellent, as was veteran actor, and one of Wayne's closest personal friends, Bruce Cabot.

John Wayne has never claimed to be a great actor and, indeed, he usually plays only himself on the screen. But who ever asked more of him than simply to entertain us with the kind of red-blooded action we craved? I certainly didn't, and most of the kids who sat with me through all those films on their original releases didn't either. John Wayne was the right man at the right time to help make my young moviegoing days so memorable.

Above: The publicity blurb accompanying this shot from *Stagecoach* (United Artists 1939) stated that "Wayne has received Hollywood's 'big break' of 1938." How right that was! *Left:* Wayne and Anna Lee in a quiet moment from *Seven Sinners* (Universal 1940).

Top: In one of the most spectacular fights in screen history, Wayne and Randolph Scott went at it in a remake of *The Spoilers* (Universal 1942). Although Wayne and Scott did much of their own work, stunt men Alan Pomeroy and Eddie Parker filled in during the long shots. *Right:* Wayne and Albert Dekker slug it out in *In Old California* (Republic 1942).

Right: A gagged-up publicity portrait for *In Old Oklahoma* (Republic 1943) with Wayne and Martha Scott. This film has been retitled recently as *War of the Wildcats. Below:* Raymond Massey, Ray Milland, and Wayne were the brawling stars of the Cecil B. DeMille epic sea adventure, *Reap the Wild Wind* (Paramount 1942). Wayne played the villain who sank his own ship on a reef, accidentally killing Susan Hayward.

Above: Wayne and Gordon Jones, *right*, warn daredevil John
Carroll that planes are scarce in *Flying Tigers* (Republic 1942).
Below: Anna Lee and John Carroll talk things over with
Wayne prior to his taking off on a mission in *Flying Tigers*
(Republic 1942). That's Chester Gan in the plane's cockpit.

Above: Wayne gets some friendly advice from Charles Winninger in *A Lady Takes a Chance* (RKO 1943). *Below*: Wayne and Randolph Scott engage in a little clowning around early in *Pittsburgh* (Universal 1942) with Shemp Howard, but they wind up a few reels later having another classic slugfest.

Above: Wayne, Claire Trevor, and Roy Rogers escape from their captors in
Dark Command (Republic 1940). *Below:* It doesn't look as if Wayne is really
frightened by Ward Bond or his gun in *Dakota* (Republic 1945).

Above: Dennis O'Keefe and Wayne seem to be fighting World War II in front of a process screen in *The Fighting Seabees* (Republic 1944). *Right:* Ray Middleton and Wayne in another brawl, this time in *Lady from Louisiana* (Republic 1941).

Opposite page: Wayne leads another heroic charge in *Back to Bataan* (RKO 1945). *Above:* Wayne challenges LeRoy Mason to "make his play" in *Angel and the Badman* (Republic 1947). *Right:* Wayne with Sigrid Gurie in *Three Faces West* (Republic 1940).

Right: Ward Bond and Wayne did most of their own stunts in *Tall in the Saddle* (RKO 1944). *Below:* Wayne and Walter Brennan in *Red River* (United Artists 1948). This was one of Wayne's all-time best performances.

Above: Wayne had a few psychological problems in *Wake of the Red Witch* (Republic 1948), besides obvious romantic problems with co-star Gail Russell. As in *Reap the Wild Wind* (Paramount 1942), Wayne went to a watery grave with a sunken ship. *Right*: Wayne was at his best in the remake of *Three Godfathers* (MGM 1948).

12.

The Horn of Plenty

By this time you must think I spent almost my entire moviegoing young life wallowing exclusively in a sea of routine cinema bilge, with only an occasional journey to see those great classic presentations of the forties. Let me put your minds at ease by saying that of course I went to see probably hundreds of other films during this remarkable decade in film history. However, a film book five times this size could not do justice to those great quality products such as *Casablanca, Mrs. Miniver, Yankee Doodle Dandy, Sergeant York, This Gun for Hire, For Whom the Bell Tolls, Spellbound* and so many others. My intention has been to present a picture of what moviegoing was like for an adventurous-minded boy living in the days of World War II and frequenting the small theaters of the time. Escapism, pure and simple, was the name of the game. However, in this final chapter I would like to indulge myself to the point of including some particular highly successful big-budget films that I went out of my way to see and that gave me a great deal of pleasure.

Since we were involved in a massive war effort, it was only natural that we would find the studios turning out dozens of giant wartime spectacles. Warner Bros was producing most of these choice items with their very biggest stars (*Action in the North Atlantic* with Bogart and *Destination Tokyo* with Cary Grant were two of the best), and I found *God Is My Co-Pilot* to be a favorite in a kind of perverse sense. The film was full of all those delightful propagandistic extremes that we now squirm at. Richard Loo,

playing Tokyo Joe, was a classic example of the screen's stereotyped portrayal of the Japanese enemy, and he had a field day delivering such classic trivia lines as "All right, you Yankee Doodle Dandy. Come and get it," and "Here's some of that scrap metal you sent us, Yankee" as he fired a round of bullets at Dennis Morgan—who ultimately dispatched him in flames, delivering the line, "There's your six feet of China. Go fill it!" I guess I was also having a movie love affair with the Flying Tigers themselves, as those P-40s with the painted teeth were featured in both this film and *Flying Tigers* with John Wayne.

Comedies were also big attractions, and I went out of my way to see delightful little gems like *Sitting Pretty* in which Clifton Webb gave his remarkable performance as the genius turned babysitter, Lynn Belvedere, *The Bachelor and the Bobby-Soxer*, featuring Cary Grant in a silly role of a lawbreaker who is sentenced by judge Myrna Loy to an unpleasant task which ultimately finds him behaving like an imbecile with Shirley Temple, and *Mr. Blandings Builds His Dream House*, which found Grant again paired with Myrna Loy and involved this time in building a house in the country complicated by many hilarious obstacles.

Musicals were extremely big in those days and of particular appeal were those lavish Technicolor delights turned out by Twentieth Century-Fox featuring Betty Grable, Alice Faye, and others. Looked at today, a great many of them like *The Dolly Sisters, Song of the Islands, Diamond Horseshoe,* and *Greenwich Village* simply fail to hold up and are often quite soggy and sentimental bores. But there were several which were quite good, like *Coney Island* and *The Gang's All Here*. *Coney Island* was one of those turn-of-the-century songfests that found rivals Cesar Romero and George Montgomery fighting for the affections of Betty Grable, while Phil Silvers ("Glad to see ya!") was around for laughs. Betty never looked more gorgeous, and she sang some delightful numbers, including "Take It from There." *The Gang's All Here* had some perfectly awful acting from James Ellison, but lavish production numbers staged by Busby Berkeley and an all-star cast headed by Alice Faye, Carmen Miranda, Phil Baker (of the famous $64-dollar-question radio show *Take It or Leave It*), and Charlotte Greenwood with her high-kicking antics. Alice was in top form, also, singing "No Love, No Nothing, Until My Baby Comes Home" and "Journey to a Star." Other musical delights of the time included *Holiday Inn*, in which Bing Crosby sang his famous "White Christmas," *Higher and Higher* with a scrawny Frank Sinatra singing "A Lovely Way to Spend an Evening" and "I Couldn't Sleep a Wink Last Night," and *Hello, Frisco, Hello* with Alice Faye singing the Academy-Award winning "You'll Never Know."

The all-star production was also very much in evidence at the time. Our armed forces needed these star-laden spectaculars as morale boosters, and the studios were quick to oblige. The plots of most of these films were positively dreadful, but the appearance of star after star made up for them. *Hollywood Canteen* was a prime example, in which soldier Robert Hutton mooned over his favorite star, Joan Leslie, and bumped into everyone from Bette Davis and John Garfield (who had actually formed the *real* Hollywood Canteen) to Jack Benny and Roy Rogers. *Thank Your Lucky Stars* was another all-star mess that found Eddy Cantor playing a dual role in a "let's put on a big show" story in which Bogart, Flynn, Sheridan, Davis, and the rest of the Warner Bros' roster either did quick walk-ons or production numbers. Other mélanges included *Star Spangled Rhythm*, *Variety Girl*, and *Duffy's Tavern* from Paramount; *Thousands Cheer* from MGM; *Follow the Boys* from Universal; and *Stage Door Canteen* from United Artists.

Not only were there all-star musicals, but several interesting straight dramas emerged featuring star-filled casts. *Tales of Manhattan* was a fascinating collection of interrelated short tales which were tied together by the movement of a pair of dress tails from person to person. The most mov-

ing performance in the film was given by Charles Laughton as an orchestral conductor who finally gets his big break to lead a concert orchestra and while doing so wears the tails, which start ripping apart at the seams as the concert progresses, turning success into a bitter failure. *Flesh and Fantasy* consisted of three short stories, the most famous of which found Edward G. Robinson having his palm read by Thomas Mitchell and being told that he would commit a murder. The uncertainty of the situation drives Robinson ultimately to killing Mitchell and fulfilling the prophecy. *Follow the Boys* had George Raft and others involved in setting up USO shows, and offered some excellent little bits such as W. C. Fields's classic routines, Jeanette MacDonald's singing, and Orson Welles with his famous magic act. One of the least remembered all-star presentations was a delightful film called *Forever and a Day*, which had seven directors utilizing almost eighty famous stars and character actors to tell the story of a house through the years as it was inhabited by different owners.

There were three crime stories that I found of particular appeal. *T-Men* with Dennis O'Keefe was a taut, gripping little crime meller that had plenty of action and thrills. Wallace Ford, that great character actor, gave an excellent performance as a stool pigeon, and I can never forget the scene where he is eliminated by the mob by being locked in a steam room as they turn the heat up to full strength. *To the Ends of the Earth* had Dick Powell going all the way around the world on the trail of the mysterious head of a dope-smuggling operation, and *The Street with No Name* was another exciting crime-fighting saga, which pitted Mark Stevens against a vicious Richard Widmark, who, at the film's finale, sets up Stevens in an elaborate trap where he is to be killed by his own men, but is thwarted and mowed down by police bullets.

I even went to see such diverse material as *Kings Row*, an excellent drama which was indeed way ahead of its time and which I am sure I never appreciated fully until I saw it again many years later; *Saboteur*, a fine Alfred Hitchcock film with a shattering finale that found Norman Lloyd (who later became a producer and director) falling to his death from the upraised arm of the Statue of Liberty; *Lifeboat* (another Hitchcock vehicle), with its complex collection of all-star castaways headed by Tallulah Bankhead, and the stark drama and tragedy of *The Ox-Bow Incident*.

Even as I write these few last paragraphs the titles keep coming into my mind, and they really seem to be limitless, so I will dispense with the naming of any additional films for fear of overlooking all those obvious entries I probably should have listed.

The horn of plenty really did spill forth an abundance of screen entertainment in the years of the forties. And though we had our *Tahiti Honey, Sweethearts of the U.S.A, Hullabaloo, Pierre of the Plains,* films that few people ever saw or heard of again, there was always a *For Me and My Gal, How Green Was My Valley, Cover Girl,* and similar divertissements to compensate.

I am sure the percentage of hits as far as entertainment value is concerned was considerably greater than the product turned out today.

And for those of you who are just laying in wait out there with questions like "Why didn't you include . . ." and "How come you chose . . ." formed angrily on your lips, let me only paraphrase the statement of the storyteller in *Jungle Book* who, when asked what happened to Mowgli after the forest fire at the film's end, replied, "That is *another* story." Thus I say to all my readers that perhaps their choices may appear in some future collection—but that, my friends, is *another* book.

Left: Betty Grable and June Haver in one of the decade's gaudiest Technicolor musicals, *The Dolly Sisters* (Twentieth Century-Fox 1945). *Below:* In one of the connected stories of *Tales of Manhattan* (Twentieth Century-Fox 1942) Charles Laughton gets a set of dress tails to wear at his concert. They begin to fall apart at the seams as he begins conducting, turning his triumph into moving failure.

In this sequence from *Forever and a Day* (RKO 1943), a film that told a story
of a house through various ownerships, Ian Hunter, Sir Cedric Hardwicke, and Buster
Keaton seem to be having some difficulties.

Above: In *Flesh and Fantasy* (Universal 1943) Thomas Mitchell reads
Edward G. Robinson's future in his palm, and predicts that he will kill
someone. Mitchell turns out to be the victim. *Below:* Alan Hale, *right*, tries
to convince Dennis Morgan that there is a guiding "force" that helps
them in battle in *God Is My Co-Pilot* (Warner Bros 1945).

Above: Bing Crosby and Bob Hope hoked it up in a little golfing routine in the all-star *Variety Girl* (Paramount 1947). *Right*: Barbara Hale and Frank Sinatra were two of the stars in *Higher and Higher* (RKO 1943).

A sequence in the star-laden review *Star Spangled Rhythm* (Paramount 1942)
found Fred MacMurray, Lynn Overman, Ray Milland, and Franchot Tone doing a skit
lampooning women at a card game.

Right: Mark Stevens and Lloyd Nolan look down at the bullet-riddled body of Richard Widmark in *The Street with No Name* (Twentieth Century-Fox 1948). *Above:* One of the sequences in *Follow the Boys* (Universal 1943) had Orson Welles doing his magic act. *Left:* Charlie Grapewin and George Raft were two vaudeville hoofers who formed USO tours in *Follow the Boys* (Universal 1943).

Above: Robert Cummings was the innocent victim
of persecution in *Saboteur* (Universal 1942).
Below: Betty Grable in a production number from
Coney Island (Twentieth Century-Fox 1943).

Left: Gypsy Rose Lee was one of the all-star guests in *Stage Door Canteen* (United Artists 1943). *Above:* Wallace Ford, *left,* was the informer and Dennis O'Keefe an undercover Treasury Department agent in *T-Men* (Eagle-Lion 1947).

Above: Alice Faye, Phil Baker, and Carmen Miranda were the stars of *The Gang's All Here* (Twentieth Century-Fox 1943), a glossy Technicolor musical with numbers staged by Busby Berkeley. *Opposite page, top:* Reissues of *The Wizard of Oz* (MGM 1939) with Judy Garland, Jack Haley, and Ray Bolger never failed to attract packed matinee houses. *Opposite page, bottom:* Dick Powell tracked down the mysterious head of a dope-smuggling ring in *To the Ends of the Earth* (Columbia 1948). Here he is with Vladimir Sokoloff, *left,* and Peter Chong.

Above: Bette Davis was one of the real-life founders of, and a guest star in, *Hollywood Canteen* (Warner Brothers 1944). *Opposite page, top:* John Boles and Gene Kelly are two more stars who wanted to form entertainment units for our servicemen, here seen in *Thousands Cheer* (MGM 1943). *Opposite page, bottom:* Bing Crosby and Marjorie Reynolds starred in *Holiday Inn* (Paramount 1941), the film in which Crosby introduced the song "White Christmas."